STUDIES IN HISTORY, ECONOMICS AND
PUBLIC LAW

Edited by the
FACULTY OF POLITICAL SCIENCE
OF COLUMBIA UNIVERSITY

NUMBER 539

THE IMPACT OF THE UNDISTRIBUTED PROFITS TAX
1936-1937

BY

GEORGE E. LENT

THE IMPACT OF THE UNDISTRIBUTED PROFITS TAX 1936–1937

BY

GEORGE E. LENT, Ph.D.

Associate Professor of Economics
University of North Carolina
Chapel Hill

NEW YORK
COLUMBIA UNIVERSITY PRESS
LONDON: OXFORD UNIVERSITY PRESS
1948

PRINTED IN THE UNITED STATES OF AMERICA

Published in Great Britain and India
by
GEOFFREY CUMBERLEGE
OXFORD UNIVERSITY PRESS
London and Bombay

TO CHARLOTTE

PREFACE

Few episodes in American tax history have been more significant than that of the undistributed profits tax. Enacted in 1936, it was effectively repealed in 1938 after a brief but eventful life of only two years. While perhaps no other Federal tax measure has had a more profound effect on existing practices and policies of business, and few have had such broad implications for the economy at large, no adequate inductive study has ever been made of this experience. It is the purpose of the present study to fill this gap.

Repeal of the undistributed profits tax left unsolved the problem of reconciling a proportional tax on corporation income with a progressive income tax on individuals. While there is little likelihood that the undistributed profits tax will be reenacted, at least in its previous form, a study of its effects (and defects) should provide a more informed and enlightened approach to the integration of our present unsatisfactory dual income tax system.

The method employed in this study is essentially statistical in character. It is based primarily on data made available by the U. S. Treasury Department in the Statistics of Income, Statistics of Income Source Book, and other published and unpublished reports to which the author had access. In addition, reports of the Securities and Exchange Commission, Temporary National Economic Committee, and of the Department of Commerce have been heavily drawn upon. The results of several contemporary industry questionnaires were also found useful in the study.

I wish to thank Professor Robert M. Haig for his many helpful suggestions on points of interpretation and style. I also wish to thank Professor John B. Woosley, University of North

Carolina, for his kind interest and exchange of views which clarified many ideas. Grateful acknowledgment is also made to Professors Arthur R. Burns, James C. Bonbright, and Dr. William Vickrey, Columbia University, and to Professor Henry Oliver, Northwestern University, for their constructive criticism of various sections of the manuscript.

GEORGE E. LENT

UNIVERSITY OF NORTH CAROLINA
CHAPEL HILL
MAY 29, 1947

CONTENTS

CHAPTER VI

CHAPTER VII

CHAPTER VIII

CHAPTER IX

CHAPTER I

LEGISLATIVE HISTORY OF THE TAXATION OF UNDISTRIBUTED PROFITS

1. LEGISLATIVE DEVELOPMENTS BEFORE 1936

RECOGNITION of the corporation as a legal entity apart from its shareholders has presented one of the most serious obstacles to the progressive taxation of individual incomes since the inception of the income tax in the United States. Many attempts had been made to reconcile their inherent conflicts and inequities but it was not until the enactment of the surtax on undistributed profits in 1936 that any radical attempt was made by the Congress to integrate the separate taxes on corporations and individuals. The enactment of this measure can be best understood in the light of its legislative history over a period of many years.

THE CIVIL WAR INCOME TAX

The Civil War income tax evidenced a more rational approach to the taxation of income than the practices of the present day. In regarding the individual as the proper object of income tax, the corporate entity was either ignored where practicable, or taxed as the source of personal gain. As a result, tax discrimination between the individuals and the corporation was virtually avoided. Shareholders of mercantile and industrial corporations were taxed at graduate rates on their pro rata share of corporation earnings, whether distributed or not. However, in the case of quasi-public corporations such as banks, insurance companies, railroad and canal companies, a flat rate of tax was collected from the corporation on interest and dividend payments as well as upon retained earnings.[1] The only tax on the corporation as such, however, was that remaining on undistributed profits because of the opportunity

[1] *Act of June 30, 1864*, Public No. 148, 38th Cong., 1st Sess., Ch. 173, Secs. 116-122.

of deducting the rate from dividend and interest payments.[2] Tax duplication was avoided by the exclusion of such dividends and interest from the taxable income of individuals. Since the tax collected at the source was a flat rate of 5 per cent (with the revenue act of 1864) and the personal rate was graduated from 5 per cent to 10 per cent on net incomes over $10,000, the possibility existed of an appreciable differential in favor of the taxation of dividend income so treated. This situation was remedied in 1865, however, by an amendment which required stockholders to include dividends in their taxable income but entitled them to receive a credit for the tax withheld from the corporation.[3]

The Civil War income tax thus attempted coordination of the personal income tax with that on the corporation by two different methods, both of which have since been advocated as solutions for present-day difficulties. One of these was the partnership method which ignored the corporate entity of the typical industrial and trade corporation; the other bore some similarity to the tax credit device which was first adopted as an essential feature of the modern income tax, and remained in effect from 1913 to 1935.

THE TAX CREDIT DEVICE

The Revenue Act of 1913 excluded dividends from the normal tax on individuals, since dividends were taxed at the same rate, one per cent, as part of corporation net income.[4] The Revenue Act of 1916 increased the normal rate to 2 per cent for both corporations and individuals. With the amendment to the Revenue Act of 1916 in 1917, however, the equivalence between these two rates was abandoned by the

2 As a matter of practice corporations generally assumed the entire tax themselves without withholding it from the bondholder or stockholder. To that extent, it became a tax on the corporation. E. R. A. Seligman, *The Income Tax* (New York: the Macmillan Co., 1921), p. 515.

3 *Act of March 3, 1865*, 38th Cong., 2d Sess., Ch. 78.

4 Sec. II, par. b.

imposition of an " additional " tax of 4 per cent on corporation income. Since 1916 the corporation normal tax has always exceeded the normal tax on individuals, to which the tax credit on dividends was limited. This tax credit device was finally eliminated in 1936 with the adoption of the tax on undistributed profits.

Some students of the subject have advanced the theory that the corporation income tax until 1921 was, in principle, a device for the collection of personal income taxes at the source, rather than a tax on corporations as such.[5] While there is some evidence of this rationale, which found a precedent in the Civil War income tax, the integration of the two was actually limited to the normal tax for which a tax credit was given to the shareholder on dividend income received. The Act of 1913 and succeeding laws, however, provided for " additional " rates on individual net income which had no equivalence with the corporation rate. Moreover, as we have seen, the corporation normal rate actually exceeded the normal individual tax beginning with 1917. Unlike true taxation at the source, as it is practiced in Great Britain, for example, no refunds were made to dividend recipients for taxes collected in excess of their liabilities. Finally, dividend income was reported for tax purposes net of tax paid by the corporation, instead of being included in the individual's net income.

TAXATION OF UNDUE ACCUMULATION OF PROFITS

The disparity between the flat normal tax on corporation income and " additional " graduated rates on individual incomes was recognized as a major problem from the inception of the income tax in 1913. These surtaxes were first imposed on individual incomes in excess of $20,000 and ranged up to 5 per cent. In order to minimize the opportunities for tax evasion by the retention of corporation income, shareholders

5 See for example, the *Preliminary Report of the Committee of the National Tax Association on Federal Taxation of Corporations*, Robert Murray Haig, Chairman, Oct., 1938, p. 7.

were required to include in their personal incomes their pro rata share of profits in corporations " formed or fraudulently availed of " for the purpose of avoiding the additional rates.[6] Use of personal holding companies and accumulation of earnings beyond the reasonable needs of the business was *prima facie* evidence of fraudulent intent. This provision was retained in substantially similar form by the Revenue Acts of 1916 and 1918 and has had a continuous existence in one form or another up to the present time, its lineal descendant being Section 102 of the Internal Revenue Code.

The Revenue Act of 1921 replaced the mandatory partnership method with a penalty tax of 25 per cent on the entire net income of the corporation itself which was formed or availed of for the purpose of tax avoidance.[7] This penalty was increased to 50 per cent by the Revenue Act of 1924, and was retained at this rate with the revisions of both 1926 and 1928. In lieu of this surcharge and all other taxes on the corporation, however, the 1921 Act gave stockholders the option of declaring their distributive share of profits if all consented. This provision was eliminated in 1924 but restored in 1926 and 1928 with respect to the penalty tax only. In 1934 the tax on undue accumulations (Section 102) was graduated at 25 per cent and 35 per cent on net income *retained* of less than or more than $100,000, respectively; thus credit was given for dividends distributed, unlike the previous acts which assessed the entire net income whether or not distributed in part.

The foregoing legislative attempts to prevent tax avoidance by administrative action were admitted to be generally ineffective because of the difficulty of proving the " purpose " to avoid taxes. Until 1928 the penalty provision produced practically no revenue, and since that date great difficulty has been experi-

6 *Revenue Act of 1913*, Sec. II, par. A(2).

7 Sec. 220.

enced by the Bureau of Internal Revenue in enforcing it.[8] Despite the fact that the Revenue Act of 1939 finally placed the burden of proof on the corporation, it is understood that only approximately one half of the additional assessments imposed by the Bureau of Internal Revenue have been successfully collected. What "scarecrow" effect this provision may have had is difficult to determine.

After 1934 many of the worst cases of tax avoidance were cleared up by enactment of the surtax in personal holding companies, in lieu of the surtax provided by Section 102.[9] These holding company provisions were greatly strengthened and the rates increased by the Revenue Act of 1937.

COMPENSATORY TAXES ON UNDISTRIBUTED PROFITS

The above measures were concerned primarily with the elimination of tax avoidance arising from undue retention of corporation earnings. Concurrently with these penalty provisions, various attempts have been made to coordinate taxes on corporation income with those on individuals, either by ignoring the corporate entity of by imposing a special compensatory tax on retained income.[10] Since these measures originated from the basic disparity between corporation and individual tax rates, it is difficult to differentiate in principle between the purpose of eliminating tax avoidance as such and the preservation of equity in the tax system by the coordination of individual and corporation rates.

The 1917 Act imposed the first specific tax on undistributed profits which was levied on the corporation and not on the shareholder. This was a tax on 10 per cent on net income which remained undistributed six months after the end of the taxable

8 *Hearings before the Committee on Ways and Means, Revision of Revenue Laws*, 1938, p. 11.

9 Sec. 351, Title I-A.

10 The term "compensatory tax" refers to a tax rate on retained income which will yield approximately the same amount as the taxation of these earnings in the hands of the stockholders.

year, but did not apply to profits actually invested, needed for the reasonable requirements of business, or invested in United States securities issued after September, 1917.[11] A family resemblance to the above penalty taxes is apparent.

The first significant synthesis of corporation and individual income taxes was found in the Revenue Act of 1918. Personal service corporations were removed from the provisions of the normal and excess profits tax on corporations and, in lieu of these, shareholders were taxed directly on their distributive shares of income whether distributed or not.[12] A personal service corporation was defined as one whose capital was not a material income producing factor but whose income was derived from the activities of its principal stockholders.[13] Special treatment of personal service corporations remained in effect for 1919 and 1920, and survived the Revenue Act of 1921, after which it was abandoned. This marked the first and only unequivocal instance since the Civil War where the corporate veil was brushed aside and shareholders taxed in their individual capacities as partners in an incorporated business. While this method has been employed since, its application was not compulsory but subject both to the unanimous consent of shareholders and the discretion of the Commissioner of Internal Revenue.[14]

Repeal of the wartime excess profits tax was slated in the Revenue Act of 1921 and a general overhauling of the income tax system appeared to be in order. By this time increasing attention was focused on the problem of eliminating the disparities between individual and corporation income taxes which favored the stockholder. The foremost advocate of reform

11 Section 1206(2).

12 Sections 231(14); 304(a).

13 Section 200.

14 It is interesting to note that the partnership approach to the problem was recommended by the *Final Report of the Committee of the National Tax Association on Federal Taxation of Corporations*, Robert Murray Haig, Chairman, Oct., 1939, p. 24.

was T. S. Adams, former Chairman of the Advisory Tax Board in the Bureau of Internal Revenue and tax adviser to the Treasury Department. In his testimony before the Committee on Ways and Means he proposed a tax of 20 to 25 per cent on undistributed profits which he estimated would equalize the rate on unincorporated businesses, if the excess profits tax were repealed.[15] Secretary of the Treasury Houston officially recommended this solution in his annual report for the year 1920.[16] He emphasized the serious inequities which existed between the normal corporation rate of 10 per cent and personal surtaxes ranging up to 70 per cent, and concluded that, unless a compensatory tax were placed on corporations equal to the surtax placed on reinvestment income of other taxpayers, a heavy premium would be given to corporation shareholders to evade their due share of income taxes.

Several alternative methods were proposed by the Secretary, one being a 20 per cent flat tax on undistributed income and another being a requirement that corporation shareholders apply the progressive income tax rates to their pro rata share of corporation profits up to a maximum of 20 per cent. "The object of these suggestions," he declared, "is to establish so far as possible an exact equivalent between the taxation of corporation stockholders and other taxpayers. The undistributed profits tax appears to be one practicable means of obtaining approximate equality of treatment."[17] Certain disadvantages and objections were recognized. If they proved overruling, it was suggested that the excess profits tax be replaced in part by a compensating surtax on all corporation profits at a flat rate.

As a result of the growing sentiment for reform of the corporation income tax, an amendment to the Revenue Bill of 1921 was introduced in the Senate which would impose a graduated

15 *Hearings on Revenue Revision, 1920-1921*, p. 1.

16 *Annual Report of the Secretary of the Treasury*, 1920, pp. 39-43.

17 *Ibid.*, p. 40.

surtax ranging from 8 to 56 per cent on undistributed earnings. The amendment was defeated, however, and the normal rate of 10 per cent was retained for 1921. This rate was increased to 12½ per cent for succeeding years, against which a personal normal income tax credit was allowed for dividends received. Since the individual normal rate was 4 per cent on the first $4,000 and 8 per cent on amounts over, and surtax rates reached a maximum of 50 per cent, the advantage in favor of corporation income was apparent.

In 1924, Senator Jones of New Mexico introduced an amendment to the revenue bill which would supplement the existing system of corporation taxes with a tax on undistributed profits. This amendment provided for the reduction of the normal corporation rate from 12½ per cent to 9 per cent and the imposition of a surtax on profits retained in excess of 10 per cent, graduated from one quarter of one percent on 10-11 per cent retention to a maximum of 40 per cent on profits retained in excess of 59 per cent of distributable net income.[18] The measure was passed by the safe margin of 43-32 in the Senate but was rejected by the House of Representatives because of the opposition of business interests.

In 1926-27 a careful study of the problem was made by the Joint Committee on Internal Revenue Taxation which advised against introducing a surtax on undistributed profits.[19] The committee was apparently influenced by the fact that the disparity between corporation and personal income rates was no longer serious enough to warrant any radical revision of tax policies. In fact, a tendency to disincorporate for tax reasons was noted. By this time the maximum individual surtax rate had been reduced to only 20 per cent compared to a corporation rate of 13½ per cent. The committee suggested but did not recommend a tax credit for dividends paid in order to encourage distribution of unnecessary surplus.

18 *HR 6715*, 68th Cong., 1st Sess., in the Senate of the U. S., pp. 85-93.

19 *Report of the Joint Committee on Internal Revenue Taxation*, 1927, vol. I, p. 54.

The Revenue Act of 1932 seriously tipped the balance in favor of corporation taxes by increasing the rate to only 13¾ per cent compared with sharp increases all along the line in individual surtax rates up to a maximum of 55 per cent. This situation revived interest in the fundamental inequity of the income tax system which discriminated against individual proprietorships and partnerships in favor of corporation shareholders whose net income could be retained in the business without incurring the additional surtax burden. The disparity was further accentuated in 1934 when the surtax rates were stepped up sharply in the middle income brackets, with a maximum rate of 59 per cent on incomes over $1,000,000. The Revenue Act of 1936 further increased individual surtax rates which reached a peacetime peak of 75 per cent.

2. The Revenue Act of 1936

THE PRESIDENT'S RECOMMENDATIONS

The proposal to tax undistributed profits was suddenly announced by President Roosevelt in a special message to the Congress, March 3, 1936.[20] Despite several attacks on large corporation earnings in various messages of the President, no hint of the forthcoming tax program could be clearly inferred from either the revenue message of June, 1935 or his budget message of January, 1936. The Treasury Department, however, had undertaken intensive studies of the problem early in the Administration and had outlined a proposed bill to implement the program.

The President's tax program was precipitated by two unusual developments which seriously upset the proposed 1937 Budget as transmitted only two months previously, on January 3, 1936. The processing taxes, which had been enacted to underwrite the cost of the Agricultural Adjustment Act, were in-

20 *Message from the President of the United States Transmitting Additional Information Concerning the Budget for the Fiscal Year 1937*. H. Doc. No. 418, 74th Cong., 2d Sess.

validated by the Supreme Court only one month after the annual budget message.[21] Approximately $500,000,000 in revenue was required annually to support this program. In addition, passage of the Adjusted Compensation Payment Act, which authorized the payment of the veterans' bonus in 1936 instead of 1945, added an annual charge of $120,000,000 to the $160,000,000 already provided to amortize the cost over a period of nine years. Thus, an additional $620,000,000 had to be supplied in more or less permanent new tax revenue in order to offset the loss of the processing tax and to meet the additional cost of the bonus payment not previously anticipated. An additional $517,000,000 deficiency in revenue was estimated for the fiscal year 1936 by reason of the loss of processing tax receipts. In order to meet this loss it was proposed to recapture the "windfalls" resulting from the repeal of the processing tax, and to spread any deficiency over two or three years by a new excise tax on agricultural products.

The tax on undistributed profits of corporations was not proposed as a temporary measure, however, but represented a revolutionary change in the corporate tax system which would tap sources of income hitherto untouched. While the immediate occasion for the introduction of this new tax was the necessity of raising new revenue, the tax on undistributed profits was dictated by more fundamental considerations than simple revenue expediency. As we have seen, it represented the culmination of a long movement to achieve important tax reform by the removal of major inequalities in the tax system and the stoppage of certain leaks in surtaxes. President Roosevelt stated that it was designed "to provide a fairer distribution of the tax load among all the beneficial owners of business profits whether derived from unincorporated enterprises or from incorporated businesses and whether distributed to the real owners as earned or withheld from them."[22] Secondly, it

21 *United States* v. *Butler*, 297 U. S. 1 (1936).

22 *Message from the President of the United States*, *op. cit.*

was designed to remove the inequality in corporate taxes on earnings going to low income recipients and on the shares of stockholders who could afford to escape high surtaxes by withholding distribution of earnings. The details of the plan were not disclosed in the tax message but the Treasury Department had carefully worked out a measure which was calculated to achieve the desired ends.

THE HOUSE BILL

On March 26, the Subcommittee on Ways and Means presented a report supporting the President's proposal.[23] In view of the subsequent drastic modification of this plan by the Congress, it is well to review briefly the original committee recommendations, to trace the evolution of the proposal and to see how its principles were finally compromised.

The proposed tax on undistributed profits would replace the conventional normal tax on corporation net income as well as the capital stock and "declared value" excess profits taxes. The rate schedules, applied to the entire net income of the corporation, were graduated with the percentage of net income retained. Corporations distributing all of their income would be free of taxes. Preferential rates were prescribed for small income corporations (with incomes of less than $10,000) which ranged from one per cent on net incomes of which 10 per cent remained undistributed, to 29.7 per cent on incomes of which 70.3 per cent or more was retained. The effective tax rates on corporations with net income in excess of $10,000 were as follows:

Per cent of income undistributed	Tax rate
0	0
10	4
20	9
30	15
40	25
50	35
57½	42½

23 *Hearings*, Committee on Ways and Means, *Revenue Act of 1936*, March 30, 1936, pp. 4-11.

Thus, a corporation which retained 30 per cent of its net income would pay the same effective rate on its profits to which it was then subject under the 15 per cent normal tax.[24] Companies retaining in excess of 57½ per cent would be faced with a maximum rate of 42½ per cent on their entire net income.

In contrast with the final bill, the original proposal allowed dividend credit for distributions made in the period between two and one-half months after the beginning of the taxable year and two and one-half months after the close. Provision was also made for carryover of dividends declared in excess of income for the taxable year. It was recommended that all dividends be subject to normal as well as to surtax, and that dividends declared out of pre-1936 earnings be fully taxable; the customary deduction allowed for dividends received from other corporations was also eliminated.

Relief was provided for corporations with accumulated deficits in excess of profits for the year, so that a corporation would not be penalized for failure to pay dividends out of capital. Also, corporations with *bona fide* contracts prior to January 1, 1936 which prohibited or restricted the payment of dividends out of net income were exempt from the surtax for the amounts so limited. In lieu thereof, a tax of 22½ per cent was proposed on the amount of such earnings.

THE COMPROMISE OF CONGRESS

Three minor amendments introduced by the full Committee on Ways and Means left the original subcommittee bill substantially intact and it was accepted in this form by the House of Representatives with little debate. However, the more conservative Senate Finance Committee was very critical of the administrative proposal. So sharply divided was it on the merits of the "radical and complicated" bill that only two of the twenty members put up a determined fight for its principles;

24 The existing normal tax credit to individuals on their dividend income would, however, be abolished.

but even these two favored a considerable modification of the tax schedule. The majority report of the Committee, it is true, retained a flat tax of 7 per cent on undistributed income but superimposed this on a normal corporate income tax with rates three points higher than the 1935 Act. It retained the capital stock and "declared value" excess profits taxes also, at 1935 rates. The Senate finally adopted the majority bill with several amendments introduced on the floor, and the measure was sent to conference committee.

The bill which emerged from conference was a compromise measure which retained both the House principle of graduated surtax on undistributed profits and the Senate's demand for continuation of the normal tax on corporate net income as well as the capital stock and excess profits tax. This hybrid bill was finally adopted by both Houses toward the end of the session. Apparently no one was entirely satisfied with the measure but a majority accepted it as a reasonable solution which would provide some experience with a new and untried principle of taxation yet retain the conventional corporation tax which had proved a dependable source of revenue for almost twenty-five years.

PRINCIPAL PROVISIONS OF THE ACT

The graduated normal tax on net income was retained, with rates graduated from 8 per cent on income not over $2,000; 11 per cent on amounts betwen $2,000 and $15,000; 13 per cent on net income between $15,000 and $40,000; and 15 per cent on the excess over $40,000. The capital stock tax rate was reduced from $1.40 to $1.00 for each $1,000 of capital stock. The rate of the "declared value" excess profits tax remained unchanged, ranging from 6 per cent on net income between 10 per cent and 15 per cent of the adjusted declared value of capital stock to 12 per cent of the net income in excess of 15 per cent of the adjusted declared value.

The rate of surtax on undistributed profits was graduated with the percentage of the adjusted net income that remained undistributed at the end of the taxable year. "Adjusted net income" was defined as net taxable income less normal tax and interest on certain Government obligations.[25] Credits were allowed for taxable dividends paid and for amounts subject to contracts restricting dividends; specific credits were granted corporations with income of $50,000 or less.

The amount of the surtax levied was the sum of the following rates on successive portions of the adjusted net income retained:

Per cent of adjusted net income retained	Tax rate
Up to 10	7 per cent
10-20	12
20-40	17
40-60	22
Over 60	27

The dividend credit was allowed only for taxable dividends paid in cash, in kind, obligations, stock or stock rights.[26] Whereas the original proposal allowed an additional period of two and one-half months, credit was now limited to distributions actually received by stockholders in the taxable year. However, provision was made for a two year carry-over of dividends paid in excess of adjusted net income, to a year of undistributed net income.[27]

The specific credit for corporations with an adjusted net income of $50,000 or less provided for a deduction equal to the portion of the undistributed net income which was in excess of 10 per cent of the adjusted net income but not in excess of $5,000.[28] The amount of the specific credit was subject to a tax of 7 per cent instead of the surtax rate which otherwise would have been applicable.

25 Sec. 14(a).

26 Sec. 27 (a), (c), (d), (e).

27 Sec. 27 (b).

28 Sec. 14 (c).

The credit in cases of dividend contracts was limited to corporations with bona-fide written contracts made prior to May 1, 1936 which prohibited or restricted the payment of dividends.[29] Credit was also granted for an amount based on net income which was required to be set aside for payment of a debt, to the extent it was actually set aside in a sinking fund or paid out. However, only one or the other of these credits was allowable.

Exemption from the surtax was provided for commercial banks, corporations in bankruptcy and receivership, insurance companies, foreign corporations, corporations deriving a large portion of income from United States possessions, those organized under the China Trade Act of 1922, and Joint Stock Land Banks.[30]

EFFECTIVE RATES OF THE SURTAX

It was declared not to be the original intent of the Administration to force the distribution of all corporation earnings, but to impose a compensatory tax on the undistributed profits so that the Federal government would " . . . not be unreasonably and inequitably deprived of necessary revenues." [31] To accomplish the objective, the rates were devised so that " . . . additional revenue will be obtained from higher corporation income taxes, roughly corresponding to the average of the rates that would have been paid by their shareholders if corporations' earnings were fully distributed." [32]

Both as originally proposed and finally adopted, the rate schedule attempted to provide for the practical requirements of business. Under the original bill, for example, a large corporation could retain 30 per cent of its profits without paying more than the existing corporation rate of 15 per cent on its

29 Sec. 26 (c).

30 Sec. 14 (d).

31 Statement by Commissioner of Internal Revenue before the Committee on Ways and Means, *Hearings, Revenue Act of 1936*, p. 22.

32 *Ibid.*, p. 21.

entire net income. The differential rates on small incomes were even more favorable. The final surtax adopted was, of course, appreciably less onerous than that originally suggested. The graduated normal tax was still retained, but it was deducted from net income before the surtax was applied. While the maximum surtax rate was 27 per cent on that portion of earnings retained in excess of 60 per cent, the average effective maximum rate on 100 per cent retention was only 20.5 per cent; including the normal tax, the maximum rate on net profits was about 32.4 per cent. Because of the graduated normal rate and specific credit the burden on small corporations was even less. The effective surtax rate paid on adjusted net income was 7.5 per cent if 50 per cent of available earnings were retained; including normal tax, the total effective rate on corporation earnings was not in excess of 21.4 per cent.[33] The price paid for retention of 30 per cent of net income was only 3.6 per cent of net income after normal tax; and not more than 18.1 per cent including normal tax

3. Repeal of the Undistributed Profits Tax

Despite the fact that opposition to the undistributed profits tax rapidly accumulated, the year 1937 passed without any revision. The Revenue Act of 1937 was devoted almost entirely to stopping the loopholes for tax avoidance by domestic and foreign holding companies and by exchanges of property at a loss between members of the same family, or closely held corporations and trusts.

By 1938, however, any serious attempt to retain the undistributed profits tax was abandoned. While the Subcommittee on Ways and Means favored the retention of the principle of the tax, it reported out a considerably watered-down version

33 Since the surtax was based on adjusted net income after deduction of normal taxes of 15 per cent, the effective surtax rate on corporation profits was 85 per cent of 7.5 per cent, or 6.375 per cent. Added to 15 per cent gives a total effective rate of 21.375 per cent with 50 per cent distribution.

of the existing statute.[34] It provided for complete exemption from the surtax of corporations with net incomes below $25,000. It was proposed to increase the normal tax to 20 per cent for corporations with incomes of more than $25,000, with a credit for dividends paid which would result in a maximum reduction of four per cent of net income. At this time the "consent dividend" principally was introduced. This provision allowed credit to be taken by corporations whose stockholders gave written consent, filed with the Commissioner, to include in their taxable income specified amounts of earnings not actually distributed. The Committee also added a new section, the so-called "third basket," which was aimed at closely held corporations with incomes of $40,000 or more. Under this provision, corporations owned by ten or fewer persons, with certain exceptions, would be subject to a penalty tax of 20 to 30 per cent on undistributed profits.[35] The Committee bill was successfully maneuvered through the House, with the exception of the "third basket" provision which was rejected.

The Senate rejected the principle of the undistributed profits tax in its entirety. In conference, however, the House succeeded in salvaging its innocuous version which was limited by the Senate conferees to a period of two years—1938 and 1939. The amount of tax credit for dividends varied with the percentage of earnings distributed but the maximum rate was only 2½ per cent, compared to the 27 per cent surtax in the previous law.

The President refused to endorse the bill emasculating the tax on undistributed profits, and it became law without his signature. When the Revenue Act of 1939 came up for debate, he insisted upon continuation of the dividend credit principle but finally submitted to its expiration on condition that the

34 *Hearings*, Committee on Ways and Means, *Revision of Revenue Laws, 1938*, pp. 16-28.

35 *Ibid.*, pp. 28-34.

penalties for undue accumulation of corporate surpluses be greatly strengthened. The dividend credit device was then removed from the Treasury program as a psychological irritant to business recovery from the recession of 1938. At the same time, however, the standard rate of the normal corporation tax was retained at 19 per cent, without the credit.

The Congress thus allowed the bitterly contested undistributed profits tax to expire on December 31, 1939, in accordance with the Revenue Act of 1938. The tax survived four years but had never achieved the full status its proponents desired. For the first two years, 1936 and 1937, it formed part of a hybrid corporate tax structure, with somewhat modified rates. Only a remnant of the tax survived the latter two years, when the maximum rate of dividend credit was fixed at 2½ per cent. Whereas the original proposal would have replaced all existing corporate taxes with *effective* rates on net income up to 42.5 per cent, depending on the percentage of profits retained, the final version represented a surtax with *marginal* rates up to 27 per cent. Together with the normal tax, the maximum effective rate on corporation net income was only 32.4 per cent.

The effects of the undistributed profits tax on corporation enterprise and the economy in general have never been fully examined. While several valuable analyses were undertaken at the same time, the full record of its impact was not yet available.[36] It is the purpose of the following sections to make a statistical analysis of this record, so far as practicable, for the purpose of formulating conclusions which may be relevant to the taxation of undistributed profits in the future.

36 One of the most valuable inductive studies was that conducted by W. L. Thorp and E. B. George, "An Appraisal of the Undistributed Profits Tax," *Dun's Review*, September, 1937. Another less comprehensive analysis is to be found in M. Slade Kendrick, *The Undistributed Profits Tax*, Brookings Institution, Washington, D. C. (1937). The study of Alfred G. Buehler, *The Undistributed Profits Tax* (New York: McGraw Hill Book Co., 1937), is largely historical and deductive in character.

CHAPTER II

EFFECT OF THE SURTAX ON THE DISTRIBUTION OF CORPORATION EARNINGS

1. Distribution of Income Tax Returns by Surtax Rates

THE TAX BASE

In 1936, 190,141 corporations with net income reported $8.9 billion net profits; in 1937, 192,028 net income companies reported $9.6 billion (see Table No. 1). Of these corporations, 9,010 in 1936 and 10,834 in 1937 were specifically exempted from the surtax on undistributed profits tax as banks, insurance companies, corporations in receivership, China Trade corporations, etc., thereby leaving a net taxable income of $8.6 billion and $9.2 billion, respectively. In each of these years the income available for dividends, after deduction of Federal normal and "declared value" excess profits taxes, amounted to $7.6 billion and $8.1 billion. After allowance for dividend credits and non-taxable income, the retained net income remaining subject to the surtax on undistributed profits was approximately $1.2 billion in 1936 and $1.4 billion in 1937.

The surtax liability reported on the remaining tax base amounted to $145,000,000 in 1936 and $176,000,000 in 1937. The undistributed profits tax thus averaged only 1.7 per cent of net income reported by corporations subject to the surtax in 1936 and 1.9 per cent of that reported in 1937; and amounted to 13.2 per cent and 13.8 per cent, respectively, of the total Federal corporation income tax liability of these companies in each of the two years.

RETURNS PAYING NO SURTAX

In 1937, 46,349 returns, or 25.6 per cent of the total number, escaped payment of the surtax entirely through full distribution

TABLE NO. 1

RETURNS AND NET INCOME SUBJECT TO THE SURTAX
1936-1937

	1936		1937	
	Number of returns	Amount (Millions)	Number of returns	Amount (Millions)
Returns with net income [1]	190,141	$8,941	192,028	$9,635
Returns not subject to surtax [2]	9,010	382	10,834	433
Returns subject to surtax	181,131	8,559	181,194	9,202
Normal and excess profits taxes		950		1,100
Balance	181,131	7,609	181,194	8,102
Dividend paid credit [3]		6,315		6,699
Undistributed net income [4] ...	135,904	1,161	134,845	1,383
Surtax paid	135,904	145	134,845	176

Source: *Statistics of Income for 1936 and 1937.* These data are necessarily preliminary and unadjusted for subsequent audit revisions by the Bureau of Internal Revenue.

[1] Net income for excess profits tax computation for 1936 excludes 13,020 fiscal year returns not filed under Revenue Act of 1936.

[2] Returns exempt by law from the surtax on undistributed profits.

[3] Dividend paid credit plus credit for contracts restricting payment of dividends.

[4] Adjusted net income less the dividends paid credit and the credit for contracts restricting the payment of dividends. The adjusted net income equals net income for excess profits tax less: excess profits tax, interest received on certain governmental obligations, normal tax and certain other credits allowed holding company affiliates.

of earnings or credit for contracts restricting dividends. These corporations accounted for 39.4 per cent of the total corporation net income reported in this period (see Table No. 2).

Except for corporations with net income under $10,000 there does not appear to be any significant difference among the various income classes with respect to the proportion of companies avoiding payment of the surtax. Only 19.2 per cent of the returns in the lowest income class (under $5,000) paid no surtax. Since the class contains two-thirds of the total number of returns, the percentage is heavily weighted by this group. Excluding this class, the proportion of companies paying no surtax averaged 38 per cent, ranging between 34.7 per cent for the $5-10,000 income class to 43.3 per cent for the highest income class. Except for the smallest income class, there does not appear to have been any definite relationship, therefore, between the size of the income and the opportunity

TABLE NO. 2

NUMBER OF CORPORATIONS SUBJECT TO SURTAX ON UNDISTRIBUTED PROFITS, 1937

CLASSIFIED BY HIGHEST SURTAX RATE PAID

(Net income classes and money figures in thousands of dollars)

Net income class [1]	Returns subject to surtax [2]	No Surtax [3] No.	Percent	7 per cent rate No.	Percent	12 per cent rate No.	Percent	17 per cent rate No.	Percent	22 per cent rate No.	Percent	27 per cent rate No.	Percent
Under $5	119,805	23,208	19.2	96,777	80.8	....	...	....	...	....	...	....	...
5- 10	18,611	6,465	34.7	7,320	39.4	1,658	8.9	1,945	10.4	1,223	6.6	....	...
10- 15	9,150	3,471	38.0	2,959	32.4	510	5.6	559	6.1	673	7.4	978	10.7
15- 20	5,697	2,278	40.0	1,560	27.4	428	7.5	471	8.3	270	4.7	690	12.1
20- 25	3,879	1,546	39.8	933	24.1	300	7.7	435	11.2	209	5.4	456	11.8
25- 50	9,282	3,759	40.5	1,676	18.0	808	8.7	1,215	13.1	794	8.6	1,030	11.1
50- 100	6,046	2,409	39.8	830	13.7	600	9.9	949	15.7	602	9.9	656	10.9
100- 250	4,620	1,792	38.8	600	13.0	442	9.6	728	15.8	545	11.8	513	11.1
250- 500	1,819	696	38.3	240	13.2	168	9.2	303	16.7	237	13.0	175	9.6
500-1,000	1,071	390	36.4	148	13.8	148	13.8	189	17.6	109	10.2	87	8.1
1,000-5,000	974	411	42.2	147	15.1	115	11.8	161	16.5	92	9.4	48	4.9
5,000 and over	240	104	43.3	38	15.8	42	17.5	40	16.7	12	5.0	4	1.7
Total	181,194	46,349	25.6	113,228	62.4	5,219	2.8	6,995	3.9	4,766	2.6	4,637	2.5

Source: Derived from *Statistics of Income for 1937*, Bureau of Internal Revenue, U. S. Treasury Department. Part 2, pp. 11-15.

1 " Net Income " is the net income for excess profits tax computation.

2 Returns with net income not exempt by law from the surtax on undistributed profits.

3 Returns with no undistributed net income on which the dividend paid credit and/or the credit for contracts restricting dividend payments equal or exceed adjusted net income.

of corporations to avoid the surtax completely by payment of dividends or other dividend credit.

RETURNS PAYING A MAXIMUM RATE OF SEVEN PER CENT

By far the greatest number of corporations paid a maximum tax of 7 per cent. All together, 113,228 returns, or 62.4 per cent of the total, limited their "undistributed" net income to less than 10 per cent of the adjusted net income (see Table No. 2). The explanation of this situation is to be found in the operation of the specific credit provision of the law which permitted corporations with adjusted net income below $50,000 to take a specific credit equal to the portion in excess of 10 per cent of the adjusted net income, but not greater than $5,000. The specific credit taken was assessed at 7 per cent instead of the higher rate to which it might have been subject for the proportion of earnings not actually distributed. As a result, 80 per cent of the smallest income companies and 39 per cent of the $5-10,000 class limited their maximum surtax to 7 per cent. Because of the limitation of the specific credit to companies with adjusted net income of less than $50,000, the percentage of returns paying a maximum surtax of 7 per cent leveled out about this range to 13-15 per cent of the total.

RETURNS PAYING A MAXIMUM SURTAX OF 27 PER CENT

At the other end of the scale, only 4,637 returns, 2.5 per cent of the total and accounting for 4.7 per cent of net income reported, paid a maximum surtax rate of 27 per cent. In general, this meant that credits received for the payment of dividends, contracts restricting payment of dividends, and specific credit, amounted to less than 40 per cent of their adjusted net income.

Above the $10,000 net income class there does not appear to be any significant difference with respect to the percentage

1 The following analysis is limited to the year 1937. Statistically, the experience for 1936 was very similar and, therefore, does not warrant separate treatment.

of corporations paying the maximum surtax rate, until the million dollar corporation is reached. Between incomes of $10,000 and $1,000,000 the proportion paying the maximum rate varied from 12.1 to 8.1 per cent. Of the 1,214 returns reporting net income above $1,000,000, however, only 52 companies, or 4.2 per cent, and only four companies with net income in excess of $5,000,000, paid the maximum surtax rate of 27 per cent.

It seems apparent, therefore, that the burden of the surtax itself fell most heavily on the middle class of corporations with incomes ranging from $10,000 to $1,000,000. Except for the benefit of the specific credit on very small incomes, two explanations may tentatively be offered for this situation: Either there was less compulsion to escape the direct tax on undistributed profits by reason of the tax savings to the shareholders, or less ability to avoid the tax by reason of the greater urgency of reinvesting earnings. Because of the difficulty of evaluating these factors which existed in varying degrees among corporations of various size, the objective evidence of tax paid provides no adequate measure of the impact of the surtax on corporations. The compulsion to distribute the entire earnings may have entailed a sacrifice equal to that measured by the maximum surtax rate; on the other hand, payment of the maximum surtax may have presented the less onerous alternative. These factors will be examined more carefully below.

2. Effect of the Tax on Aggregate Net Dividend Payments

It is generally recognized that the undistributed profits tax had a considerable influence on corporate dividend policy in 1936 and 1937. The magnitude of this influence, however, has never been fully measured; nor can it be measured except in terms of probabilities. While there is an accurate record of dividends paid in these years, there is no knowledge of what the amount of the dividends would have been without the tax.

One student of the subject has maintained that dividends were not materially increased by the surtax. Based on a correlation of the percentage of dividends to profits with an index of trade activity over a long period of years, he concluded that the law did not cause appreciable change in corporation dividend policy.[2] Because of the failure of this investigation to substantiate the popular opinion that dividends were in fact measurably increased, it was suggested that, ". . . students of public finance ought to evaluate the recent American experience with a tax on the undistributed profits of corporations in terms of its efficiency as a revenue measure, and not as a reform measure." [3]

The validity of the statistical approach employed in this study is seriously open to question. While the size of dividends may indirectly be a function of "business activity," they are more directly and uniquely related to earnings available. The correlation of the *percentage* of earnings distributed with business activity, therefore, ignores the magnitude of the net income from which the distribution is made, except in so far as it is reflected in the volume of business. Because of the equivocal nature of the relationship presented in the scatter diagram, one critic came to the conclusion from the same data that dividends did not increase at all but actually declined.[4]

With the returns all in for succeeding as well as for prior years, it is possible to estimate with considerable reliability the real effectiveness of the surtax in impelling a distribution of corporation earnings in 1936 and 1937. For this purpose, the dividends paid out by all corporations (excluding dividends received) were correlated with net profits after income taxes

2 Francis McIntyre, "The Effect of the Undistributed Profits Tax Upon the Distribution of Corporate Earnings—A Statistical Appraisal," *Econometrica*, vol. VII, No. 3, July, 1939, p. 345.

3 *Ibid.*, p. 348.

4 Harry G. Guthmann, "The Effect of the Undistributed Profits Tax upon the Distribution of Corporate Earnings; a Note," *Econometrica*, vol. VIII, October, 1940, p. 354.

(excluding dividends received) for several years preceding and following the period under study, 1936-37. In order to get a reasonably stable period of time which has not influenced unduly by either the depression or the war, and yet sufficiently long in duration to establish a statistical relationship, the years prior to 1934 and after 1942 were omitted.[5] By 1942 it is apparent that the capital requirements for plant expansion and other wartime considerations were beginning to curtail the distribution of corporate profits.

Based upon deviations from the relationship derived above, the net amount of dividends paid in cash and other assets that can be attributed to the effects of the surtax on indus-tributed profits is estimated at approximately $1.1 billion for each of the years 1936 and 1937 (see Table No. 3). These were dividends received by individuals, partnerships, trusts and other non-corporate stockholders that would probably not have been received in these years but for the surtax. Compared to the probable volume of dividends normally expected for the level of corporation profits in these years of between $3.4 and $3.5 billion, as shown by Table No. 3, the amount of $1.1 billion represents an increase of approximately one third. This estimate confirms the more commonly accepted belief that dividends in this period were substantially greater than they would have been without the undistributed profits tax. In this respect the tax can hardly be said to have failed as a " reform " measure. The question of its " efficiency " as a tax measure will be examined below in more detail.

3. Increases by Major Industry Groups

Considerable variations were experienced by different types of industries with respect to the relative amount of increase in

5 The years 1936 and 1937 were, of course, also excluded from the data correlated.

TABLE NO. 3

ACTUAL AND "EXPECTED" NET DIVIDENDS PAID BY ALL CORPORATIONS—1934-1942

Year	Net Dividends Paid [1]		
	Actual	"Expected" [2] (billions of dollars)	Difference
1934	$2.55	$2.39	$ + 0.16
1935	2.77	2.89	− 0.12
1936	4.52	3.42	+ 1.10
1937	4.63	3.51	+ 1.12
1938	2.92	2.84	+ 0.08
1939	3.60	3.54	+ 0.08
1940	3.83	3.80	+ 0.03
1941	4.29	4.16	+ 0.13
1942	4.12	4.17	− 0.05

Source: U. S. Department of Commerce, *Survey of Current Business*, April, 1946.

[1] Excluding intercorporate dividends.

[2] Derived from second degree equation of correlation between net profits after Federal and State income taxes (x) and net dividend payments by domestic corporations (y) for years 1934-1942 excluding 1936 and 1937: $y = \$2.20 \text{ billion} + 0.356x - 0.0154x^2$.

the dividends attributable to the surtax. An analysis by major industrial classification is shown in Table No. 4.

This table excludes the record of financial corporations such as banks, insurance companies, investment companies, holding companies, brokers and similar corporations. Since these corporations are to a great extent beneficiaries of American industry and trade, through their extensive investment in common and preferred stocks, it is believed desirable to eliminate the effect of the flow of intercorporate dividends through their hands in order to determine more accurately the economic sources of the income distributed by manufacturing, trade, transportation, mining, communication, public utilities and other types of activities. These non-financial corporations accounted for about 98 per cent of net dividend payments by American industry in 1936-1937. The effect of the flow of these dividends on the distribution of earnings by financial corporations is reserved for later discussion.

TABLE NO. 4

ESTIMATED INCREASE IN NET DIVIDENDS[1] DISTRIBUTED BY NON-FINANCIAL CORPORATIONS

(Millions of Dollars)

Industry	1936				1937			
	Net dividends		"Extra" dividends		Net dividends		"Extra" dividends	
	Actual	"Expected"[2]	Amount[2]	Percent increase	Actual	"Expected"[2]	Amount[2]	Percent increase
All Corporations	$4410	$3420	$990	29%	$4530	$3460	$1070	31%
Manufacturing	2322	1652	670	41	2345	1663	680	41
Trade	643	412	230	56	603	401	200	50
Communication & Public Utility	649	650	0	0	692	667	25	4
Transportation	287	235	50	21	287	230	55	24
Mining	192	197	—5	—3	257	242	15	6
Real Estate	173	142	30	21	197	145	50	34
Services	70	55	15	27	78	60	18	30
Agriculture, Forestry & Fisheries	36	19	17	90	29	18	11	60
Construction	36	21	15	70	42	22	20	90

Source: United States Department of Commerce, *Survey of Current Business*, April, 1946.

[1] Intercorporate dividends eliminated.

[2] Since these are approximations only, estimated from linear functions for the most part, the sum of the individual groups do not add up to the total.

MANUFACTURING

Manufacturing corporations contributed over one half of net dividend payments by non-financial corporations in this period. As a result of the surtax it is estimated that dividends of this group were increased by the remarkably uniform rate of 41 per cent in each of the two years. In general, dividends paid by manufacturing corporations were fairly responsive to business profits over the period—for every $100 increase in profit, an average of $23 was distributed, compared to $19 for all non-financial corporations (see Chart). It is somewhat surprising, therefore, that this group of companies should have distributed a proportionately greater amount under pressure of the tax than industry generally.

WHOLESALE AND RETAIL TRADE

The pressure on trade corporations for the distribution of earnings was appreciably greater than in the case of manufacturing or any other major segment of business. As a result of the surtax it is estimated that this group of corporations increased their dividends on the average by 53 per cent, with slight variations between the two years. This effect was even more significant when the conservative dividend policy of trade companies is considered (see Chart). Normally this group of companies distributed only $13 for each $100 increase in earnings realized during the base period, compared with $19 for all non-financial corporations, $23 for manufacturing and $35 for mining companies.

COMMUNICATION AND PUBLIC UTILITIES

The undistributed profits tax had no discernible net effect on the distribution of earnings by public utility and communication companies in 1936; total dividends were about what could be expected from the level of earnings in this year. In 1937, some slight increase of about 4 per cent is noted. It should not be inferred, however, that many public utility com-

CORPORATION NET PROFITS AND NET DIVIDENDS

1934-1942

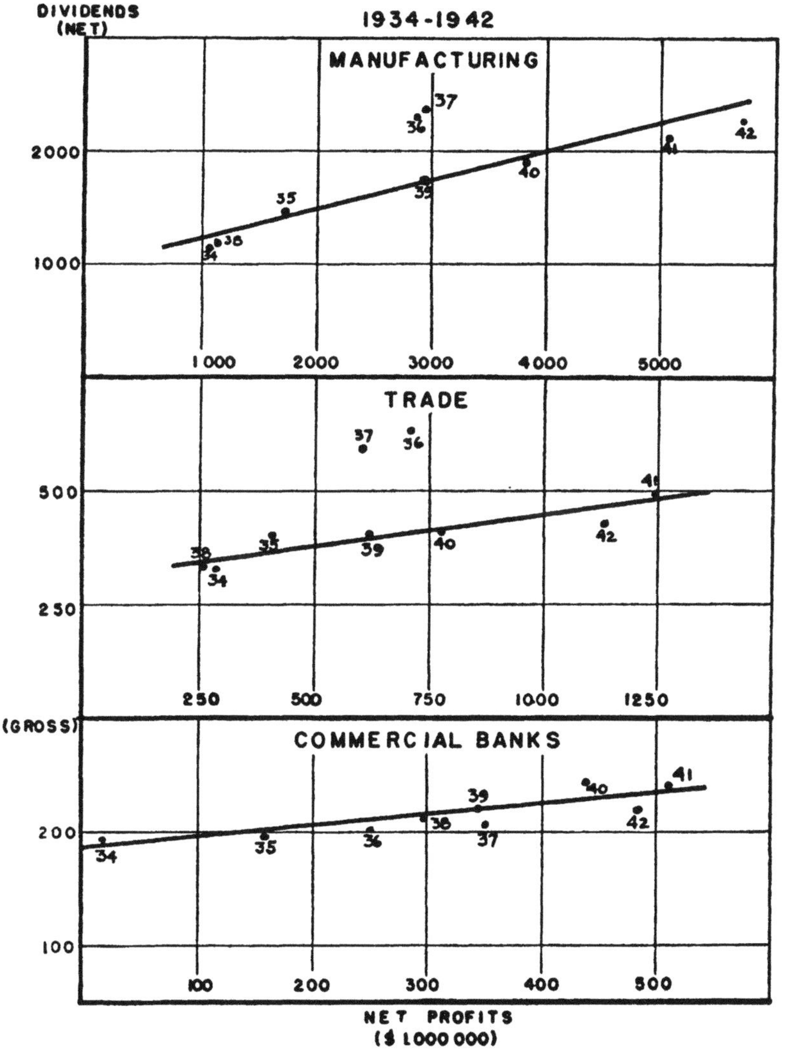

SOURCE: DEPARTMENT OF COMMERCE

panies did not greatly increase their dividend payments. Such increases were offset by a reduction in dividend payments by others, with the result that very little or no net increase was evidenced for the group as a whole.

TRANSPORTATION COMPANIES

The increase in dividends by companies engaged primarily in transportation is estimated at about $50-55 million for the period, a rise of 21 and 24 per cent, respectively, for 1936 and 1937. The estimates for transportation companies are subject to somewhat greater error than for other classes of business. In 1935, particularly, net dividend payments exceeded those of any other year in the period studied. Pipe line companies were responsible for this spurt which is unexplainable on the basis of available earnings alone. If this experience is ignored, the relationship of dividends to net profits available in other years appears to be in line with expectations, with the exception of 1936 and 1937 when the undistributed profits tax contributed to rather generous distributions.

MINING AND QUARRYING

The net effect of the undistributed profits tax on dividend payments by mining companies was negligible. In 1936 net dividends were actually below expectations; in 1937 they exceeded expectations by about 6 per cent.[6] As explained below (pp. 46, 47), the failure of the surtax to induce a significant change in dividend policy is more apparent than real since the industry totals conceal a significant readjustment of dividend policies among its different members. Because of the liberal depletion allowances permitted by law, mining corporations were in a particularly favored position which enabled them to distribute their statutory net income without an undue sacrifice of capital. While a large segment of the industry actually increased dividends appreciably, these tended to be offset by curtailed distributions of the larger companies, leaving little net change.

6 Industry dividends have normally been very responsive to earnings, a factor which may partly account for the relatively slight deviations in 1936 and 1937. On the average, dividends have increased $35 for every $100 increase in earnings during this base period.

REAL ESTATE

Generally, dividend payments by real estate companies were remarkably stable and showed virtually no correlation with net income available; in the base period, dividends increased on the average only $2 for each $100 increase in net profits (i.e., reduction in net loss). In 1936 and 1937, however, the effects of the surtax are clearly seen; dividends exceeded normal expectations by about 21 per cent in 1936 and about 34 per cent in 1937. The increase was not so substantial as that of the manufacturing or trade group but was, nevertheless, significant in consideration of the fact that the industry as a whole experienced a net loss of from $150,000,000 to $200,000,000 in these years.

SERVICES, INCLUDING AMUSEMENTS

Appreciable increases in dividends were realized by the service group of corporations in 1936 and 1937, amounting to about 27 per cent above normal in 1936 and 30 per cent in 1937. The largest part of this is attributed to the motion picture industry. While it is estimated that net dividend payments expanded by $15,000,000 to $18,000,000, the relationship between net income and dividends is less clearly defined for this segment than for other industrial classes. The impact of the undistributed profits tax is, nevertheless, clearly seen.

AGRICULTURE, FORESTRY AND FISHERIES

Although small in dollar amount, the increase in dividends for this group of corporations was proportionately greater than for any other industry class except the construction industry. In 1936 the increase in dividends attributable to the undistributed profits tax is estimated at $17,000,000, or 90 per cent above expectations; in 1937 the increase was about $11,000,000, or approximately 60 per cent greater than normal.

CONTRACT CONSTRUCTION

The percentage increase in dividends experienced by this business group was approached only by agricultural corporations. In 1936 approximately 70 per cent more earnings were distributed than probably would have been paid out in the absence of the surtax; in 1937 dividends were enhanced by an estimated 90 per cent. Because of the small size of the industry these increases represented only a small contribution to the total, about $15,000,000 in 1936 and $20,000,000 in 1937.

Dividends of Financial Corporations

all financial corporations[7]

The net income of financial corporations is derived to a great extent from the net profits of other corporations. For this reason, dividend payments are shown gross rather than net as in the analysis of non-finance companies. That is, dividend income received is included in both the net profits and dividends paid estimates of the Department of Commerce, employed in this analysis.

It is estimated that the net increase in dividends paid out by this group of corporations as a result of the undistributed profits tax was approximately $300,000,000 in 1936 and $220,000,000 in 1937. Because of the relatively poor relationship between profits and dividends, this estimate is subject to an appreciable margin of error.

It will be noted that the sum of the net increase in dividends for the non-financial and financial group of companies aggregated approximately $1.3 billion for each of the years 1936 and 1937, about $0.2 billion greater than the net increase in dividends of $1.1 billion estimated for all corporations. This difference may be largely accounted for by the absorption of non-financial dividends by financial corporations. This is particularly

7 This group of companies includes banks, investments, trusts, holding companies, commercial credit and finance companies, industrial and personal loans, insurance agents, brokers, life and other insurance companies. While real estate companies are classified in this group by the Department of Commerce, they are treated as non-financial companies for the purposes of this analysis.

true of investment and holding companies included in the latter group.[8]

BANKS AND TRUST COMPANIES

Since banks and trust companies were exempted from the surtax on undistributed profits, no significant variation in dividend payments from their normal relationship to profits should have been experienced, in theory. A "control" group is thus conveniently provided by which the experimental results of the subject corporations can be effectively validated. It is particularly significant to this inductive inquiry, therefore, that commercial banks actually paid out slightly less dividends than expected in the years 1936 and 1937 (as shown by Chart). Further confirmation is thereby made of the influence of tax policy on the distribution of corporation earnings.

4. Distribution by Size of Corporation

ALL NET INCOME CORPORATIONS

The percentage of earnings distributed normally varies directly with the size of the corporation. In the two year periods immediately before and after the undistributed profits tax (i.e., 1934, 1935, 1938 and 1939), the average percentage of available net income distributed by all corporations earning profits was 76.7 per cent. The percentage distributed by the largest corporations, however, was about 85 per cent—just double that paid out by the smallest asset class, 43 per cent.[9]

8 In 1936 these companies (i. e., "finance n. e. c.") received dividends from other corporations amounting to $1,468,000,000 and paid out $1,380,000,000; in 1937 they received $1,510,000,000 and distributed $1,428,000,000. *Survey of Current Business*, April, 1946, pp. 16, 18.

9 See Table No. 5, compiled from Statistics of Income for these years. Net income available for dividends was computed from "compiled net profits" after deduction of income taxes. Because of the distortion introduced in the smallest asset class in 1934 when the percentage distributed was 92 per cent, comparison is made with the next largest asset class, $50,000-$100,000, which experienced only minor variations in dividends paid out in the years 1934, 1935, 1938 and 1939, the base period employed for purposes of comparison.

During the surtax period, the average distribution was raised to 83.3 per cent, an increase of 8.6 per cent over the base period.[10] The most striking feature of this increase, in which we are particularly interested, was its unequal distribution with respect to size of corporations. Although the proportion distributed still varied directly with the size of the corporation, the relative increase in the percentage of earnings paid out by small corporations was substantially greater than the increase for large companies. Small companies which distributed only 43 per cent in the base period paid out 69 per cent in 1936-1937, and increase of 60 per cent; the largest class, on the other hand, increased its average distribution only 9 per cent. The range between the small and large corporations was consequently narrowed from a margin of 100 per cent to only 33 per cent.

The declining rate of increase in the percentage of earnings distributed by intermediate size corporations is readily apparent from Table No. 5. Corporations in the $10-50 million asset class actually experienced a reduction from 85.8 per cent to 82.9 per cent in the relative amount of earnings distributed. This paradox points up the conceptual limitation of the analytical approach employed and which is taken into account in

10 Apparent discrepancies from the foregoing data (pp. 33-41) with respect to the percentage change in dividend distribution are accounted for, in large part, by differences in the data employed. These differences are as follows: (1) Only corporations reporting net income are included, instead of all corporations; (2) the net income figures are those compiled in Statistics of Income from income tax returns reported to the Treasury Department and do not reflect upward audit adjustments subsequently made by the Bureau of Internal Revenue which were taken into account by the Department of Commerce; (3) the data represent taxable net income and not economic income as defined by the Commerce Department which eliminated all depletion allowances and capital gains and losses; (4) finally, dividends received are not eliminated but included in the income available for dividends paid out; the Department of Commerce eliminated intercompany dividends for the purpose of determining the net economic income attributable to different industry sources. (See Gardner F. Derrickson, "The Trend of Corporate Profits, 1929-45," *Survey of Current Business*, April, 1946, pp. 9-12, for a technical description of these data.)

TABLE NO. 5

PERCENTAGE OF DIVIDENDS TO NET INCOME AVAILABLE [1] BY SIZE OF CORPORATION
SURTAX PERIOD COMPARED TO NON-SURTAX PERIOD, 1934-1939
Selected Major Industrial Groups

Industry	Period	Under $50	$50 to 100	$100 to 250	$250 to 500	$500 to 1000	$1000 to 5000	$5000 to 10,000	$10,000 to 50,000	Over 50,000	Total
All Net Income Corporations	1934-1939 [2]	54.1	42.9	48.5	56.0	61.6	68.9	72.9	85.8	84.9	76.7
	1936-1937	64.7	69.0	73.8	74.9	73.0	73.8	76.6	82.9	92.4	83.3
	Ratio	1.20	1.61	1.52	1.34	1.19	1.07	1.05	0.97	1.09	1.09
All Manufacturing	1934-1939 [2]	40.6	37.9	42.9	49.9	56.9	64.7	68.7	77.6	79.2	70.7
	1936-1937	58.9	66.4	69.7	71.4	92.2	70.0	72.9	80.9	93.7	81.5
	Ratio	1.45	1.75	1.62	1.43	1.62	1.08	1.06	1.04	1.18	1.15
Trade	1934-1939 [2]	30.3	36.2	38.7	51.5	55.7	64.8	67.1	79.7	74.1	61.8
	1936-1937	51.4	62.5	69.0	72.8	72.9	70.7	79.2	84.6	85.6	75.6
	Ratio	1.70	1.73	1.78	1.41	1.31	1.09	1.18	1.06	1.16	1.22
Mining and Quarrying	1934-1939 [2]	90.9	80.7	76.8	86.9	88.0	102.4	109.6	126.8	114.2	108.3
	1936-1937	113.7	101.7	102.8	105.9	100.8	102.6	98.1	109.5	95.9	101.8
	Ratio	1.25	1.26	1.34	1.22	1.15	1.00	0.90	0.86	0.84	0.94
Construction	1934-1939 [2]	16.5	25.1	32.3	39.6	40.8	47.2	73.4	73.3	.....	45.8
	1936-1937	46.1	63.2	68.9	71.9	71.8	82.3	80.8	54.9 [3]	.....	71.5
	Ratio	2.79	2.52	2.13	1.82	1.76	1.74	1.10	0.75	.....	1.56

Asset Size (Thousands of Dollars)

Source: Statistics of Income Source Book, Statistical Section, Bureau of Internal Revenue.

[1] Compiled net profits, including dividends received, after normal and excess profits tax but before undistributed profits tax.

[2] Excluding 1936 and 1937.

[3] Includes only 6 companies, one of which was in the $50-100,000 group.

the previous analysis of the general relationship of dividend payments to earnings. The fact that profits were considerably greater in 1936 and 1937 than the average for the base period tends to underestimate the full effect of the undistributed profits tax with respect to the comparative percenage of earnings distributed. Since the above estimates are unadjusted for size of income available for dividends, the percentage distributed in the surtax years is substantially less than it would have been if the level of profits had been equal to the average for the base period.

It is interesting to observe that the middle range of corporations with assets from $100,000 to $10,000,000 tended to approach on average distribution of about three quarters of their available income, compared to a previous range of 48.5 to 73 per cent. Apparently the forces of the undistributed profits tax tended to equalize the factors bearing upon dividend policy for the great mass of medium size businesses.

It should not be inferred from the above data that small corporations were primarily responsible for the greatly enhanced dividend payments during the period under study. The fact is that the percentage of earnings distributed by the largest group of corporations increased by the same relative amount as the average for all industry. The relatively small reduction in earnings distributed by the second largest asset class actually offset the greatly enhanced dividends by the smaller companies. Because of the great concentration of profits among large corporations, the experience of small companies, while significant in itself, was of little influence on the situation as a whole. In 1936 and 1937, net available income of the largest corporations, with assets in excess of $50,000,000, accounted for 42.5 per cent of the total; and the two largest classes, with assets in excess of $10,000,000 accounted for 61.7 per cent of the entire net income of domestic corporations available for dividends.

MANUFACTURING

Manufacturing companies as a whole experienceu a greater relative increase in the proportion of earnings distributed than the average for all industry. In 1936 and 1937 the average distribution was 81.5 per cent compared to 70.7 per cent in the base period, an increase of 15 per cent. While the greatest relative increases were found among corporations with less than $1,000,000 assets, the giant corporations actually exceeded the average for this industrial group with an increase of 18 per cent. As seen by Table No. 5, these increases were largely offset by the relatively conservative change in dividend policy of companies with assets of from $1,000,000 to $50,000,000. The giant corporations, with assets over $50,000,000, accounted for 38.7 per cent of the net income available for distribution, compared to only 13.4 per cent for companies below $1,000,000 in assets; the balance, 47.9 per cent was concentrated in the intermediate group.

WHOLESALE AND RETAIL TRADE

In 1936-1937 trade corporations experienced an even greater change from the base period in the percentage of net income paid out. The overall increase from 61.8 per cent to 75.6 per cent averaged 22 per cent. The change for small companies was relatively much greater than in the case of large companies: For corporations with assets below $1,000,000 the increase between the two periods ranged from 31 to 78 per cent, varying inversely with the size of corporations.

It is clear that the predominance of small and medium size corporations was responsible for the relatively greater increase in dividend payments by trade companies than was the case in manufacturing, as pointed out above (p. 36). Net income of corporations with assets below $1,000,000 amounted to 37.4 per cent of the total whereas the giant corporations accounted for only 21.8 per cent, compared to 13.4 per cent and 38.7 per cent, respectively, in manufacturing industry. Since the average increase in the dividend percentage of small companies (below $1,000,000 assets) was 53.2 per cent, the average for the industry was heavily weighed by this group.

CONSTRUCTION

The disparity is even more pronounced in the case of the construction industry, which expanded dividends more than any other industrial class of corporation (*Supra,* p. 40). The ratio of the percentage of earnings distributed in 1936 and 1937 compared to the base period ranged from 2.79 for the smallest companies to 1.74 for those in the $1,000,000-$50,000,000 asset class; and dropped to only 0.75 for the largest ($10,000,000-$50,000,000) asset class. Since 55.4 per cent of net income in 1936 and 1937 was accounted for by corporations with assets of less than $1,000,000, and 85.5 per cent by those below $5,000,000 assets, the influence of the smaller companies on the average increase of 56 per cent is apparent.

MINING AND QUARRYING

The case of this group of corporations is unique. While smaller companies tended to increase the proportion of net income distributed by as much as 25 and 35 per cent, all mining companies as a whole actually distributed a smaller proportion of 1936-1937 earnings than they distributed in the base period. As seen above (p. 38), the amount of net increase in dividends by this industry was negligible.

The explanation of this perverse relationship is undoubtedly to be found in the peculiar benefits of the tax law which provides for unusually large deductions for depletion. Whether based on a percentage or gross sales or on discovery value, these companies were automatically permitted to retain up to 50 per cent of their net income (before the deduction) for depletion allowances.[11] Since these allowances were appreciably in excess of the amount necessary to amortize the investment, this class of corporations could easily distribute up to 100 per cent of their statutory net income without sacrificing funds essential for reinvestment.

11 *Revenue Act of 1936,* Sections 23 and 114.

It is significant, therefore, that mining corporations actually distributed in excess of their statutory net income during the base period (108.3 per cent). The actual distribution by asset size ranged from 76.8 per cent to 126.8 per cent, and followed in general the familiar variation with size of corporation. Apparently as a result of the surtax, however, a curious reaction took place which clearly manifested a tendency to approach the 100 per cent credit established by the law. Larger companies previously distributing in excess of 100 per cent reduced dividends and smaller companies previously distributing less than 100 per cent liberalized their dividend policy so as to avoid the corporation surtax. The result was that the range of income distributed by asset classes in 1936 and 1937 varied only within small limits of from 96.0 per cent to 113.7 per cent compared to a range in the base period of from 76.8 to 126.8 per cent. It, therefore, seems likely that companies reducing dividend payments were motivated by the desire to avoid the taxation of undistributed profits by stabilizing dividends over a period of years. Many, of course, received a dividend carry-over which they could use in the following two years.

MAJOR CLASSES OF MANUFACTURING COMPANIES

For the purpose of testing the variation in the pattern of dividend payments among different varieties of companies within the same general species, comparison is made of selected groups of manufacturing companies (see Table No. 6). Out of five larger groups selected at random, surprising uniformity is found among four with respect to the average ratio of distribution in 1936 and 1937 to the distribution in the base period; considerable variation in the experience of different asset sizes is concealed, however, in the aggregate figures. In the case of the fifth, not only was the ratio for all companies greatly in excess of that for all manufacturing as a whole, but a strangely diverse pattern was followed with respect to the relationship of dividends to net income available by corporations of different size.

The greatest variation among corporations of different size is found in the case of *metal and its products*. The amount distributed by small companies was greatly enhanced, by as much as 100-140 per cent, declining with the size of the corporation up to the $1,000,000-$10,000,000 asset size, and then increasing again by 27 per cent for the very largest corporations. Considerable increases were also experienced by small *paper and pulp* companies, with only modest changes in the percentage of earnings distributed by the very large companies. Less extreme variations were found in the increases by asset size for *chemicals and allied products,* but the overall percentage increase (18 per cent) was greater than in the case of three other groups. More moderate variations were also found in the case of *food and kindred products,* with increases ranging from 8 per cent for large companies to 80 per cent for smaller companies.

The situation in the *liquor and beverage* industry, however was atypical: In the base period the percentage of income distributed varied *inversely* with the size of the corporation for asset classes up to $10,000,000. The industry as a whole paid out only 52 per cent of earnings compared to 70.7 per cent distributed by all manufacturing companies.

During the surtax years the average amount of earnings distributed was raised to 68.2 per cent, an increase of 31 per cent, compared to a 15 per cent increase for all manufacturing companies. Little change is noted, however, with respect to the relationship of dividends to size of corporation. The percentage increase in the proportion of earnings paid out by small companies was relatively modest (from 9 per cent to 29 per cent) compared to that of other industries; and, while relatively greater for some larger size corporations, the ratio between the two periods was actually less than 1.0 in the $5,000,000-$10,000,000 group.

The most likely explanation of this lack of conformity with the rest of the manufacturing industry is the lack of homogen-

TABLE NO. 6

PERCENTAGE OF DIVIDENDS TO NET INCOME AVAILABLE[1] BY SIZE OF CORPORATION

SURTAX PERIOD COMPARED TO NON-SURTAX PERIOD, 1934-1939

Selected Major Manufacturing Groups

Asset Size
(Thousands of Dollars)

Industry group	Period	Under $50	$50 to 100	$100 to 250	$250 to 500	$500 to 1000	$1000 to 5000	$5000 to 10,000	$10,000 to 50,000	Over 50,000	Total
Metal and its Products	1934-1939[2]	23.3	31.6	38.4	47.1	51.8	68.7	71.7	71.9	67.0	65.9
	1936-1937	56.4	63.1	66.3	65.9	60.7	64.9	68.7	74.5	83.5	75.4
	Ratio	2.42	2.00	1.73	1.40	1.17	0.94	0.96	1.04	1.25	1.14
Chemicals and Allied Products	1934-1939[2]	59.1	46.8	52.5	57.6	74.4	73.5	79.9	87.9	89.7	83.8
	1936-1937	63.8	77.2	77.0	77.8	76.8	82.0	89.4	89.9	110.1	98.5
	Ratio	1.08	1.65	1.47	1.35	1.03	1.12	1.12	1.02	1.23	1.18
Food and Kindred Products	1934-1939[2]	40.9	36.2	41.7	55.2	61.3	71.4	60.5	86.3	85.4	76.3
	1936-1937	57.3	65.2	76.3	78.6	75.8	80.9	75.2	93.2	100.0	89.4
	Ratio	1.40	1.80	1.83	1.42	1.24	1.13	1.24	1.08	1.17	1.17
Paper, Pulp and Products	1934-1939[2]	29.1	30.1	40.0	49.2	55.3	58.2	57.6	75.3	68.0	61.3
	1936-1937	54.4	64.1	64.9	63.7	69.3	64.4	81.8	73.5	70.9	70.6
	Ratio	1.87	2.13	1.62	1.29	1.25	1.11	1.42	0.98	1.04	1.15
Liquors and Beverages	1934-1939[2]	74.8	63.0	60.3	52.9	51.5	40.4	48.5	64.4	.....	52.0
	1936-1937	81.5	80.0	78.0	77.1	67.3	57.8	44.8	78.9	.....	68.2
	Ratio	1.09	1.27	1.29	1.46	1.31	1.43	0.92	1.23	.....	1.31

Source: Statistics of Income Source Book, Statistical Section, Bureau of Internal Revenue.

[1] Compiled net profits, including dividends received, after normal and excess profits tax but before undistributed profits tax.

[2] Excluding 1936 and 1937.

eity in the companies included. The major dissimilar groups in particular were the smaller and older non-alcoholic beverage industry, which had quite stabilized its growth,and the rapidly developing alcoholic beverage industry, which had been re-established only a few years previous with the repeal of prohibition. Because of their expanding capital requirements, the latter companies tended to reinvest their earnings rather than distribute them to the stockholders.[12] Since they were well represented among the larger companies, they probably account for the inverse relationship of earnings distributed to the size of company. The relatively greater amount of earnings distributed by all asset sizes in 1936 and 1937 may be ascribed to the influence of the undistributed profits tax on what have generally been closely held corporations.

5. Non-Dividend Distributions of Income

The compulsion to distribute earnings was not limited to the formal declaration of dividends. Tax avoidance was accomplished more directly through various means of reducing the amount of taxable net income declared. Considerable latitude exists in this respect, at the discretion of management, for increasing legitimate expenditures on advertising, maintenance, payment of bonuses, higher wages, and probably most important, executive salaries. Many such increases during 1936 and 1937 were attributed to the undistributed profits tax. About one half of the companies questioned in one survey reported an increase in one or more of these payments.[13]

Bonuses and increases in salaries to officers were reported for the year 1936 by 23 per cent and 26 per cent, respectively, of the sample of corporations, with some duplication of these

12 In 1937, cash dividends paid out by the non-alcoholic beverage industry amounted to 68.0 per cent of profits compared to 55.3 per cent distributed by the alcoholic beverage industry, one of the smallest percentages reported by any minor industry class. *Taxation of Corporate Enterprise*, T.N.E.C. Monograph No. 9, p. 178.

13 Thorp and George, *op. cit.*, p. 13.

two categories probable.[14] Bonuses to employees and wage increases were attributed to the surtax by 28 per cent and 23 per cent, respectively, of the respondents in this same year. Other increases reported were maintenance (13 per cent of respondents), advertising (13 per cent of respondents); obsolescence, research, and other expenditures were increased by a smaller number of the companies queried. Small companies were more responsive to increases in expenditures than large companies, with 55 per cent reporting increases compared to 52 per cent of medium size corporations, and only 41 per cent of large firms.[15]

No estimate is possible of the total aggregate increase in expenditures induced by the surtax. Nor would it be possible to isolate the effect of the surtax from other conditions in these years which tended to liberalize corporation expenditures. While such increases appear to have been a rational reaction to the taxation of undistributed profits, their importance must be discounted to some extent in consideration of the general improvement in business conditions of 1936 and 1937 which generated higher wages and bonuses and other adjustments.[16]

The advantage of the non-dividend form of surtax avoidance to the owners of small businesses in particular is clear. Because of the active participation of the owners of small businesses as managers and officers, any sharp distinction between the two forms of income received as salary for services and dividends on investment is arbitrary and unrealistic. One recent study, in fact, concluded that, " . . . in many small corporations the relationships between officers' compensation and dividend disbursements is determined as much by tax

14 *Ibid.*, p. 14.

15 *Ibid.*, p. 13.

16 For purposes of later discussion it is assumed that the amount attributable to the surtax in each of the years was at least $150,000,000 (Chapter IX).

requirements as by any other consideration."[17] Any increase in the corporation tax would, therefore, tend to stimulate increases in executive salaries, personal income taxes remaining the same. While the surtax on undistributed profits could have been avoided by larger dividend payments, the alternative form of distribution avoided the normal corporation income tax as well.

Quantitative evidence of the relative importance of increases in officers' salaries to dividend payments is provided by the record of an identical sample of 381 small manufacturing corporations selected from five different industrial classes.[18] The increases in net profits available for dividends, compensation of officers, dividend payments, and retained earnings between 1935 and 1936 are shown in the following summary:

	1935	1936	Increase
		($1,000)	
Net income	$ 238	1,190	952
Officer compensation	2,371	2,973	602
Total	2,609	4,163	1,554
Dividends	296	1,129	833
Retained earnings	1 [19]	185 [19]	184

It is apparent from these data that the absolute increase in dividends by this group of companies did not greatly exceed the increase in compensation of officers. Including executives' salaries and bonuses the total economic net income was $1,554,000 larger in 1936 than in 1935; of this amount, $602,000 was distributed in the form of compensation to man-

17 Charles L. Merwin, Jr., *Financing Small Corporations* (New York: National Bureau of Economic Research, 1942), p. 3.

18 Charles L. Merwin, Jr., *Financial Characteristics of American Manufacturing Corporations*, T.N.E.C. Monograph No. 15, Washington (1941), App. F., Tables 1-A to 1-D.

19 Discrepancy between net income available, dividends and retained earnings is accounted for by the fact that the sample includes net loss companies as well as net income companies which paid dividends.

agement compared to $833,000 paid out to stockholders. A net amount of $185,000 remained undistributed in 1936, compared to a net balance of practically nil in 1935. Because of the greatly enhanced income available in 1936 it would be fallacious to attribute the full amount of the increase in either salaries or dividends to the undistributed profits tax, but the relative proportions of these two forms of distribution are, nevertheless, indicated for small companies. It is likely that the relative amount of additional executive compensation diminished with an increase in the size of the corporation.

CHAPTER III

THE DETERMINANTS OF DIVIDEND POLICY

1. Factors Encouraging Distribution

MARGINAL RATES AND TAX AVOIDANCE

The fundamental objective of the taxation of undistributed profits is the full application of personal income tax rates to all income, whether or not arising through the corporate form of ownership. While the Revenue Act of 1936 fell far short of this ideal, it, nevertheless, radically altered the previous absolute advantage of retaining rather than distributing corporation earnings. So long as the levy on corporations was limited to the normal *ad rem* tax, the shareholder could avoid personal income taxes completely by failing to distribute earnings.[1] As a result of the surtax, the shareholder was now confronted with the problem of the *relative* amount of income which should be retained in order to minimize taxes on his equity in corporation profits.

If the marginal corporation surtax rate on income retained exceeded the marginal surtax rate on the personal income of a shareholder, dividends would tend to be distributed up to the point where the two rates were equalized. The degree of compulsion on the distribution of corporation earnings, therefore, depended generally on the relationship of the corporation surtax structure to that of the personal income tax: The higher the corporation rates in comparison with the personal income tax scale, the greater the incentive given to dividends.

Since the maximum corporation surtax rate was 27 per cent, its effectiveness was limited primarily to that area of income

1 In principle, earnings could be retained until death and be subject only to estate or inheritance taxes. In practice, however, shareholders would tend to pay dividends so as to minimize taxes over a period of time.

which was subject to a personal income tax (including normal and surtax) of 27 per cent or less. This corresponded to a gross income of $40,500 for a married person with no dependents; where the individual was also liable for state income taxes the limit was correspondingly lower. A resident of New York State, for example, would tend to limit his gross income to around $34,000 (assuming a personal exemption of $2,500).

The same marginal principle operated at lower surtax schedules, depending on the income level of the shareholder. The surtax paid by corporations on various percentages of adjusted net income distributed was less than the normal and surtax rates paid by a married person within the following gross income limits:

Per cent Distribution	Personal Gross Income
90-100	$ 6,500
80- 89	16,500
60- 79	22,500
40- 59	28,500
0- 39	40,500

In other words, taxes could be saved by distributing up to 100 per cent of corporation income if the gross income of the sole or principal owner remained below $6,500; up to 89 per cent, where the resulting personal income was less than $16,500, and so forth. Where more than one shareholder with different levels of income and share in ownership were concerned, dividends would equitably be limited to an amount where the increment in personal income taxes paid by *all* recipients was equal to the savings in corporation surtaxes. Thus, it might be expedient to distribute earnings even beyond the point where the personal income of any individual exceeded $40,500 (in certain states) if the income of the others was sufficiently below this to realize a net tax advantage. This would be particularly true of family corporations with a close community of interest. It is likely, however, that minority interests were subordinated to the tax considerations of the principal stockholders in many cases.

The potential savings realized by the retention of earnings should take into account the prospect of future taxes as well. If the investment were planned to be liquidated at some future date, the retention of earnings would tend to enhance any capital gains realized and thereby diminish the net tax savings. Moreover, dividend policy would also be influenced by prospective changes in the tax structure. If the trend of personal income taxes was believed to be upward, the relative tax advantage of current distribution might be enhanced, and *vice versa.*

SMALL CORPORATIONS

The greatly increased percentage of profits distributed by small corporations clearly reflected the premium placed on the payment of dividends by the newly established differential between the marginal rates of tax on corporations and individuals. The reaction of these companies to the undistributed profits tax can be explained by the predominant characteristics of their ownership and control, which provided both the incentive and the means to the distribution of profits for the purpose of tax avoidance.

In the past, the nature of the ownership of small and medium size corporations has been a matter of considerable speculation. Considerable light was thrown on this question by an exhaustive statistical analysis of 1936 income tax returns from which the data in Table No. 7 are summarized. These data reveal a remarkable relationship between the asset size of corporations and the income level of their owners which largely explains the radical change in dividend policies of small corporations in these years. It is apparent that the income of stockholders tends to increase with the size of the corporation as the medium size corporation is approached ($1,000,000-$10,000,000 assets); beyond this level the relationship reverses itself, reflecting the wide distribution of ownership in large listed corporations by small income individuals.

TABLE NO. 7

PERCENTAGE DISTRIBUTION OF DIVIDENDS BY SIZE OF PAYING CORPORATION AND INDIVIDUAL INCOME CLASS—1936

Asset class of paying corp. ($1,000)	Cumulative percentage of total dividends received by personal income classes:				
	Under $5,000	Under $10,000	Under $25,000	Under $50,000	Total
Under $50	28.8%	53.1%	81.2%	91.4%	100.0%
50- 100	20.3	44.7	79.4	91.5	100.0
100- 250	16.2	34.0	68.5	87.1	100.0
250- 500	13.4	27.3	58.4	82.1	100.0
500- 1,000	13.0	24.4	50.6	75.4	100.0
1,000- 5,000	12.5	22.8	42.0	62.1	100.0
5,000- 10,000	13.8	23.6	40.4	55.1	100.0
10,000- 50,000	17.1	28.6	45.6	59.3	100.0
50,000-100,000	18.4	30.3	46.9	59.2	100.0
Over 100,000	24.0	37.2	54.7	66.7	100.0
Total	18.3	31.1	51.4	67.0	100.0

Source: Derived from *Bulletin of the Treasury Department*, January, 1943, p. 6.

It is significant that about half the dividends paid out by companies with assets of $500,000 to $1,000,000 were received by individuals with incomes of less than $25,000, and that three quarters were received by those with incomes below $50,000—the critical levels above which the individual surtax rates tended to exceed the maximum corporation surtax rate. The concentration of ownership among lower income groups was even greater in the case of smaller corporations. Almost 60 per cent of the ownership of corporations with assets of $250,000 to $500,000 was limited to income classes under $25,000, with an additional 24 per cent lying between $25,000 and $50,000. Over two-thirds of the dividends distributed by corporations with assets of $100,000-$250,000 were concentrated in income groups below $25,000 and seven-eighths of their income was received by individuals with incomes under $50,000. For the smallest corporations, the concentration was even more complete, with 80 per cent of dividends received by income groups under $25,000, and 91.5 per cent by those under $50,000 income.

The adaptation of dividend policy to the personal fortunes of the individual stockholders was facilitated by the close identification of ownership with the control of small and medium size corporations. Ownership by individuals, business associates and family interests permitted the amount of dividends to be shaped readily to the income status of the individual or group as a whole. Where the controlling interest was held by one or a few individuals their personal interest in tax avoidance was probably paramount. Conflicting interests of large stockholders could be reconciled by a compromise dividend policy which tended to minimize their total taxes.

The fact that the calculus of differential tax rates on the income of shareholders determined in large part the dividend policy of small corporations, is amply evidenced in the record of small corporations.[2] The alternatives were clearly in favor of distribution and the conditions of ownership and control facilitated the process. It should not be overlooked, however, that relative tax advantage in itself was frequently nullified by many other factors which inhibited the liberality of dividend payment.

LARGE CORPORATIONS

In the case of large publicly owned corporations the tax incentives to increased dividend distribution are less apparent. It was obviously impossible to determine the relative tax advantages accruing to the wide range of incomes represented in a large body of investors whose composition was unknown and constantly changing. Moreover, the individual investor had an opportunity, through the security markets, to adjust his investments to the corporations whose dividend policy was most consistent with his best interests.[3] Large listed companies,

2 *Supra*, pp. 41-50.

3 This is known to be true in the case of the British withholding tax on corporations whose effects are not dissimilar to the tax on undistributed profits. See R. S. Edwards and D. Black, "Notes on the British Income Tax and Company Reserves," *Review of Economic Studies*, February, 1938, p. 115.

nevetheless, poured out an unprecedented flood of extra dividends.[4] Presumably this policy was dictated largely by the taxation of undistributed profits.

Directors of large corporations were probably influenced less by consideration of tax savings than by their responsibility of exercising reasonable prudence in maintaining corporation reserves. Yet, they were also responsible for economy in the conduct of corporation affairs, including the payment of income taxes which reduced the equity of stockholders.[5] The surtax on undistributed profits, therefore, undoubtedly influenced management generally to avoid any undue retention of earnings which could not reasonably be justified. In this respect, the alternative of acquiring capital from external sources was probably decisive in many instances.

In large part, dividends were probably paid at the expense of net working capital, by distributing surplus cash and other funds. While the cash balances of large manufacturing corporations increased slightly during the biennium of the surtax, liquid investments in government bonds declined appreciably.[6] Another sample of 58 large corporations shows substantial reductions in cash and marketable securities in 1936 and 1937

4 In 1937, 70.6 per cent of corporations with net incomes above $1,000,000 paid out more than 80 per cent of their earnings. *Statistics of Income for 1937*, pp. 11-14.

5 Unfortunately, the testimony on this point is very meager, and evidenced primarily in the announced purpose of issuing new shares of stock by the use of stock rights (see *infra*, pp. 119-122). In the case of the British withholding tax on corporation income, credit for which is given to shareholders by the payment of dividends, there has been considerable speculation as to its effects on distribution of earnings. The Colwyn report came to the conclusion that, ". . . when a concern is well managed, it will not be deflected by high Income Tax from sound policy in the matter of reserves." *Report of the Committee on National Debt and Taxation*, Cmd. 2800, H. M. Stationery Office, London, 1927, p. 147.

6 Friedrich A. Lutz, *Corporate Cash Balances* (New York: National Bureau of Economic Research, 1945), Appendix, p. 114.

compared with increases of a greater magnitude in 1938 and 1939, as well as a slight increase in 1935.[7]

Significant indication of the reduction in redundant funds is provided by the changing pattern of the "current ratio" experienced by 400 large companies during 1936 and 1937 as shown by Table No. 8. In practically every year, except 1937, about the same proportion of companies had a current ratio of less than 2, the conventional standard. In no year did more than 50 per cent of the companies have a ratio of between 2 and 6, except in 1936 and 1937, when almost 60 per cent of the companies were found in this group. The shift took place from companies with a current ratio of more than 6, with only 138 in 1936 and 131 in 1937 found in this group, compared to a typical number of around 180 in the good business years of 1927-1929 and in 1935. While such reduction in current ratio may be ascribed to other factors in 1936 and 1937, these same factors, e. g., the financing of increased current assets by short term loans, were also common to other years of high business activity when no such shift occurred. Such a reduction would

TABLE NO. 8

FREQUENCY DISTRIBUTION OF THE CURRENT RATIO[1] OF 400 LARGE CORPORATIONS 1927-1938

	Number of companies with current ratio:		
Year	Under 2	2 to 6	6 and up
1927	26	200	174
1928	17	208	175
1929	23	195	182
1930	18	163	219
1931	23	116	261
1932	22	112	266
1933	23	132	245
1934	19	158	223
1935	19	200	181
1936	22	240	138
1937	37	232	131
1938	23	187	190

[1] Ratio of current assets to current liabilities.

Source: Standard Statistics. Tabulated at Income Tax Study, Philadelphia. Taken from C. L. Merwin, *op. cit.*, p. 75.

7 Data compiled by the Board of Governors of the Federal Reserve System, presented by O. Altman, *Savings, Investment and National Income*, T.N.E.C. Monograph No. 37, p. 121. (See *infra*, p. 159.)

be consistent with the hypothesis that excess net working capital was distributed on account of the surtax on undistributed profits.[8]

In summary, the increased distribution of earnings by large corporations in 1936 and 1937 was probably influenced primarily by the desirability of minimizing corporation taxes *per se*. Little concern was evidenced over the comparative tax savings to shareholders or equitable apportionment of the tax burden. Such distributions were apparently made largely out of redundant cash and marketable securities whose retention as a liquid reserve could not be justified by the tax penalty.

EXCESS RESERVES ALLOWED BY LAW: DEPLETION ALLOWANCES

Mining corporations entitled to the deduction of either "percentage" or "discovery value" depletion in the determination of their taxable net income enjoyed a very privileged position under the undistributed profits tax as well as under the normal tax.[9] Because of the allowance permitted for depletion of up to 50 per cent of the net income before depletion charges, they were in effect given a substantial credit for reinvestment of their net income in excess of normal depletion allowances necessary to amortize the investment over its pro-

8 The influence of the undistributed profits tax in weakening the current ratio is suggested by one economist but other factors were believed to be more important. Charles L. Merwin, Jr., *Financial Characteristics of American Manufacturing Corporations*, T.N.E.C. Monograph No. 15, p. 69.

9 Provisions for percentage depletion permitted certain types of mining, oil and gas companies to base their depletion allowances on gross sales. The percentage allowed coal mining companies was 5 per cent, metal companies 15 per cent, sulphur mining companies 23 per cent, and oil and gas wells 27½ per cent of gross income but not to exceed 50 per cent of net income computed without such allowances. In all other cases deductions were allowed for the amortization of discovery value, or the fair market value of the mines at the date of discovery, over the economic life of the minerals, but not to exceed 50 per cent of the net income computed without such allowances. *Revenue Act of 1936*, Secs. 23, 114.

ductive life.[10] A similar benefit was given to many companies entitled to compute depletion allowances on so-called "discovery value."

The original purpose of these liberal depletion allowances apparently was to provide a stimulus to the discovery and exploration of new mineral resources. It would be erroneous to assume that mining companies actually maintain reserves equal to the depletion deductions claimed under the law. They are purely arbitrary allowances granted for the purpose of reducing taxes on earnings and bear no necessary relationship to amounts required to prevent impairment of capital.

The fact is that dividends paid in cash and other assets by all mining and quarrying companies have normally exceeded the net income earned by those reporting net income. Excluding the surtax years, over the period from 1934 to 1939 the amount of statutory net income (after taxes) reported by companies earning a net income was $691,800,000;[11] dividends paid out in cash and other assets over this same period by all companies were $938,800,000, an amount in excess of taxable profits of $248,000,000, or 36 per cent. A similar distribution was also true of 1937 when the dividends paid by net income companies exceeded statutory net income by 20 per cent.

As explained above (pp. 46, 47), this class of corporations manifested a remarkable flexibility in adjusting their dividend policy to the undistributed profits tax. They would not have

10 Actually the use of percentage depletion, rather than cost depletion, enabled many companies to cut their taxable income by more than 50 per cent because the law specifies that percentage depletion may be computed with respect to each property separately (Regulations 94, Art. 23(m)—3(h)). Exhibits of the Treasury Department show the effectiveness of percentage depletion allowances in eliminating income taxes to which the corporation would have been subject on a cost depletion basis. One case is cited of an oil company that converted a profit of $4,200,000 to a loss of $5,000,000 by reason of the excess of percentage depletion claimed in 1937. (*Hearings before the Committee on Ways and Means, Revenue Revision of 1942*, III, 3002.)

11 *Statistics of Income*; Part 2.

been able to accomplish this tax avoidance without the special depletion privilege which enabled them to reinvest real earnings without incurring the penalty of the undistributed profits tax.

As a result, the total surtax paid by this industrial class in 1937, for example, was only $5,400,000 on a taxable net income of $372,100,000 or 1.4 per cent, compared with an average surtax paid by all manufacturing industries of 2.7 per cent, and by trade corporations of 3.1 per cent.[12] If income were computed on a reasonable basis of cost depletion, the percentage of surtax was even more insignificant.

2. Factors Limiting Distribution of Earnings

GENERAL

If the distribution of 40 per cent of corporation earnings be taken as a reasonable minimum standard for dividend payments, it is significant that in 1937 only 4,637 companies out of 181,200 had a dividend credit of less than this amount.[13] The specific dividend credit, however, automatically eliminated all corporations with a net income of less than $10,000 from this category. Excluding these small companies, which accounted for 76.5 per cent of all corporations subject to the surtax, it is found that 10.8 per cent of the remaining distributed less than 40 per cent of their adjusted net income.[14] Of these, it is estimated that 1,350 corporations, or about 30 per cent, retained all of their income.

Analysis of these corporations should provide some evidence of the factors which militated against distribution of earnings. Nothing can be proved from the bare statistical data submitted in income tax returns, but certain tentative hypotheses are

12 *Statistics of Income for 1937*, pp. 63, 65.

13 See Table No. 2, *supra*, p. 29.

14 The taxable dividends of all 4,637 corporations averaged 21.4 per cent of adjusted net income; while subject to the maximum surtax rate of 27 per cent, the average effective rate was only 14.7 per cent of adjusted income. *Statistics of Income for 1937*, p. 14.

suggested by the statistics. These hypotheses are discussed below.

TAX AVOIDANCE

As pointed out above, the surtax on undistributed profits narrowed the gap between corporation and individual tax rates but fell far short of closing it up. Considerable opportunity still remained for the avoidance of high surtaxes by those in the higher income tax brackets who exercised some control over corporation policies. Analysis of 310 companies with net incomes of over $250,000 in 1937, which distributed less than 40 per cent of earnings, disclosed that three-quarters were closely held corporations, with little or no public ownership of their securities.[15]

Many of these companies were probably deterred from declaring larger dividends by other causes; but there is a strong presumption that management withheld distribution in a large proportion of cases for the purpose of tax avoidance. In the absence of complete information it is impossible to confirm this hypothesis. Some typical instances are, nevertheless, presented to illustrate the conditions under which corporations appeared able but unwilling to distribute more than a small fraction of their earnings:

A large bottling company distributed none of its earnings of $2,200,000. While net profits amounted to about 40 per cent of its total assets and half of its earned surplus, cash at the end of the year was reduced to less than $800,000. It seems reasonable to believe that a company in such excellent financial condition would have effected a substantial distribution of these earnings if the surtax of 27 per cent ($450,000 in all)

15 The company was considered to be closely held if not listed in Moody's, if it had less than 100 stockholders, or if there appeared to be an unduly high concentration of common stock ownership in the hands of one individual or family. Since only the larger companies were included, it is reasonable to assume that this percentage is greatly exceeded in the case of companies with net income between $50,000 and $250,000.

had not been less than the alternative personal income tax rate on its shareholders.

A large privately owned machine tool company had an adjusted net income of $2,400,000 but distributed only $314,000 in preferred and common dividends. The surtax paid on the balance retained was over $400,000, despite the fact that its cash on hand at the end of the year was over $2,200,000 and equal to almost 40 per cent of its total assets. Judging from its earned surplus of almost $2,000,000, it could legally have made a greater distribution without impairing its capital. While instability of earnings may have militated against greater dividends, provision could have been made to recoup additional dividends paid if there were any tax advantage to the owners.

A large department store earned $450,000 after normal taxes in 1937. Despite an earned surplus of over $3,000,000 it made no distribution to its shareholders. This corporation had a healthy cash account of almost $1,000,000 in addition to government bonds of almost $2,000,000, amounting to 20 per cent of its total assets. The fact that this corporation was closely held suggests the purpose of avoiding higher personal income taxes on its shareholders.

One of the most remarkable cases was that of a pipe line company which earned almost $500,000 adjusted net income in 1937 of which it distributed about 30 per cent, or $150,000, in dividends. This company had started only a few years previous with a capital stock of $1,000 and enjoyed unusually large profits, practically all of which were retained. By the end of 1937 the amount of cash accumulated equaled more than $1,000,000, two thirds of its total assets. While the cash was subsequently converted to "accounts receivable," the business had all the external earmarks of the "incorporated pocketbook" organized for the purpose of tax avoidance.

A well known investment banking company, which was closely held, earned $275,000 in 1937. Despite cash amounting to almost $9,500,000, 60 per cent of its assets, it paid a surtax on undistributed profits rather than pay any dividends.

Another corporation, described as an investment company, realized over $950,000 adjusted net income in 1937 but distributed only a preferred dividend of $70,000. Cash and government bonds of $2,500,000 amounted to 43 per cent of its total assets. Apparently it was more to the interest of its shareholders to pay an undistributed profits tax of $180,000 than the alternative personal income surtaxes on dividend income.

Finally, the case is cited of a large brewing company, believed to be closely held, which earned $300,000 adjusted net income in 1937. Despite a substantial earned surplus and over $500,000 in cash and government bonds, it elected to pay a premium of $62,000 for the retention of the entire amount of its earnings.

IMPAIRMENT OF CAPITAL

In a formal sense, capital is impaired when a deficit instead of an earned surplus results from the operation of a given period. In actual practice, book values do not always reflect properly the true situation because of arbitrary valuation write-ups, under-depreciation and other accounting manipulations. In principle, sound policy dictates the payment of dividends only from earned surplus (except liquidating dividends). While many states have recognized this principle in their corporation statutes, and prohibit the distribution of earnings so long as the legal capital is impaired, no cognizance of this requirement was taken by the Congress which arbitrarily fixed the accounting period at twelve months, and contrary to previous practice, allowed no offset against prior years' losses.[16]

It is of some interest to determine the influence of deficits on dividend policy under pressure of the tax. Comparison of corporations distributing all their earnings with those distributing less than 40 per cent suggests that this condition was an

16 See Chapter IV for a more complete discussion of this issue.

appreciable factor in preventing the distribution of earnings. Deficits of the former group of corporations earning more than $250,000 in 1937 amounted to about 3.2 per cent of their earned surplus, compared to about 6.1 per cent for the latter. While complete data for smaller income classes are not available for both groups, there is evidence that the ratio of deficits to earned surplus was more serious in the case of smaller corporations with meagre distribution of earnings, being about 19 per cent for the $100,000-250,000 income class.

Many other corporations were deterred from dividend payments because of their precarious financial situation. While legal capital was not impaired in a formal sense, they had just emerged from a long period of depressed earnings and deficits of the early 30's and desperately needed to build up their working capital, to rehabilitate plant and equipment which had been allowed to deteriorate, and to meet maturing obligations. Payment of an effective rate of surtax up to 20.5 per cent of adjusted net earnings represented less of a drain on their resources than payment of dividends sufficient to reduce the tax significantly and they were loath to make much, if any, distribution of earnings until their financial position was strengthened. In many instances retention of earnings was the only alternative to possible receivership and drastic reorganization which might seriously impair the equity remaining in preferred and common stock. In many cases considerable arrears in preferred stock dividends had been accumulated. These dividends were passed in 1936 and 1937 in the hope of future payments or recapitalization under more favorable conditions.

A good case in point was the Inspiration Consolidated Copper Company. This company reported earnings of $2,078,768, before surtax in 1937 of which no distribution was made.[17] Serious deficits had been incurred between 1932 and 1935 which drained its net working capital to a low of $300,000 in

17 The following data were derived from *Moody's Manual of Investments* for the appropriate years.

1935, with cash of only $146,000. Earnings were, therefore, apparently retained to restore the working capital of the company which reached $3,908,000 by the end of 1937, with cash of $1,450,000. While some dividends might have been feasible, the retention of earnings seemed to have been well advised by reason of the deficit experienced in 1938 which further curtailed working capital and reduced cash to $460,000. Moreover, notes payable to Anaconda in the amount of $7,600,000 were due in 1942, the payment of which was secured by a first mortgage on the property.

The Virginia-Carolina Chemical Corporation and the St. Regis Paper Company were in similar circumstances. Both realized a net income in 1936 and 1937 for the first time since 1932 and had accumulated sizeable arrears on their preferred stock which were subsequently settled through a recapitalization plan. Neither found it advisable to distribute earnings in 1937 (although Virginia-Carolina Chemical Corporation paid a dividend in 1936) apparently because of the desirability of conserving assets pending readjustment of the capital structure.

Many public utility holding companies were found in embarrassing situations at this time and were unable to distribute any profits realized in 1936 and 1937 to avoid the surtax. Most of these companies were capitalized at the optimistic level of earnings prevailing in the 1920's which the depressed levels of income in the 1930's were inadequate to support. Their principal difficulty was excessive pyramiding upon an equity which by 1932 had become greatly attenuated and they were forced to forego dividend payments on preferred stock in order to protect their bonds against default on interest payments. This was particularly true of American and Foreign Power Corporation which barely earned its interest in 1932, and by 1936 and 1937 had only a small margin of income which was used to pay off bank notes. By July, 1945 cumulative arrears amounted to $73.67 on 1st preferred and $103.25 on 2nd preferred stock.

The Cities Service System was in a similar situation. Due to the necessity of meeting heavy fixed charges and repaying maturing obligations, the consolidated system as a whole was forced to pay surtaxes of $3,500,000 on a taxable net income of about $21,000,000, about $850,000 of which was paid by the parent holding company. The Empire Gas and Fuel Company, one of its important subsidiaries, alone paid a surtax of about $1,000,000 upon failure to distribute any of its net income. This corporation had barely been earning its fixed charges, and by 1936 and 1937 had a slim margin of only 20 or 30 per cent. Preferred dividends remained unpaid since 1932 and were finally liquidated, only as a result of the profitable war years, in 1945.

The Consolidated Electric and Gas Company paid an undistributed profits tax of $105,000 in 1937 but reported to its stockholders a net deficit for the period after bond interest and expense. In January, 1946 its accumulated arrears on preferred stock amounted to $79.85 per share. The Cuban Telephone Company had failed to earn its bond interest between 1933 and 1936 but in 1937 $230,000 net income was realized after fixed charges. Because of its serious financial condition no dividends were paid on preferred stock, which by 1939 had accumulated to $42. At this time common stock was offered in settlement of arrears, and 93 per cent of the stockholders assented. The New York, Chicago and St. Louis Railroad Company was forced to pay a surtax of $405,000 in 1937 on undistributed earnings of almost $2,000,000. The seriousness of its condition which persisted during this period is reflected in the fact that a preferred stockholders committee was finally organized in December, 1943 to arrive at a method of liquidating the accrued dividends.

These few cases demonstrate inequality of opportunity under the law to avoid the surtax by distribution of profits. Either because of the necessity of restoring capital which had been impaired, or of avoiding further drain on liquid resources needed to safeguard payment of the corporation's liabilities, many companies had no alternative but to pay the tax. Many had weathered the great depression by following conservative financial practices (dictated in many cases by previous unsound capitalization) which were in sharp contrast to the philosophy of the surtax. While the number of companies which incurred the maximum burden of the surtax was not large, it may reasonably be inferred that the pressure on other corporations in similar circumstances to distribute earnings was frequently conducive to unwise and unjustified dividend policies.

The record of the above companies serves to point up several serious defects in the law. One was the failure to allow any carry-forward of prior years' losses, a feature which had characterized the corporation income tax law, to a limited extent at least, for many years but which was finally abandoned in 1933 with the National Industrial Recovery Act. Such a provision would have mitigated the hardship on companies recovering from business set-backs by giving them an opportunity to recover part, at least, of their losses. The second defect was the time limitation imposed on the distribution of profits within the taxable year. Failure to estimate profits accurately in advance of their realization and audit frequently exposed corporations to a penalty of 7 per cent or more on the difference not distributed. Finally, undistributed profits might be taxed twice, once by the surtax and once when such earnings were subsequently paid out. This was particularly true of the many cases where some adjustment was made in later years for cumulative arrears in preferred dividends, as frequently happened. Not only was no credit given for tax on dividends charged to earnings for the year of the undistributed profits tax but also stockholders were subject to substantially greater surtaxes when these accumulated arrears were later received in a single taxable year.

CAPITAL REQUIREMENTS

It is generally recognized that small and medium size corporations are at a disadvantage in financing their capital requirements from outside sources.[18] So far as short-term loans are concerned they have more or less ready access to the commerical banks and other financial institutions but the price paid is considerably greater than that possible to large corporations by the sale of debentures or commercial paper to banks and investment institutions. Long-term loans and sale of stock present a special problem. Most new companies are so uncertain in their prospects as to be unable to attract capital at a reasonable cost because of the risk involved. Not only may the dividend or interest rate be high but the cost of underwriting itself, including commissions, lawyers' and bankers' fees, registration costs, etc., deter such outside financing except under very favorable circumstances. Finally, sale of securities may jeopardide the control of a closely held company which prizes its independence of bankers and promoters.

For these reasons new and growing enterprises may be willing to sacrifice the premium paid for retention of earnings in order to finance their necessary capital requirements for expansion. In the absence of more definite information, it is difficult to attribute this decision to any corporation in particular. Testimony before the Congress, however, gives ample evidence that many corporations registered protests against the undistributed profits tax on this score. A survey of 3,000 companies by the Illinois Manufacturers Association, for example, indicated that 83 per cent of the respondents had delayed plant repairs, expansions, or rehabilitation because of the tax.[19] Even discounting the unfavorable reaction of businessmen to the surtax, capital improvements by small business were probably discouraged to a large extent.

18 See Chapter VII for a more complete discussion of this point.

19 *Hearings before the Committee on Ways and Means, Revenue Revision Laws, 1938*, p. 777.

Some evidence of the possible effect of new capital requirements on distribution of earnings is provided by the experience of several industries known to be expanding or requiring large capital improvements in this period. Comparison of the percentage distribution of the number of companies in industrial classes (with net income above $100,000) retaining more than 60 per cent of earnings in 1937, with their percentage distribution among all net income companies, reveals a high concentration in the brewing and distilling industry, iron and steel products, tools, and miscellaneous machinery (including machine tools). The comparative percentage distribution is shown by Table No. 9.

The most striking concentration is found in the case of the brewing and distilling industry which had its rebirth in 1933 following the repeal of prohibition. Considerable capital was required by this industry to rehabilitate plants, purchase new equipment, finance large inventories which require ageing, and to promote the sale and distribution of the product. While the

TABLE NO. 9

PERCENTAGE DISTRIBUTION OF SELECTED INDUSTRIAL CLASSES WITH DIVIDENDS OF LESS THAN 40 PER CENT COMPARED WITH PERCENTAGE DISTRIBUTION OF ALL NET INCOME CORPORATIONS

Minor industrial class	Corporations with less than 40 per cent distribution—1937 (Income above $100,000)		Per cent of all corporations with net income 1937
	Number	Per cent of total	
Brewing and distilling	32	3.89	0.27
Miscellaneous machinery .	49	5.96	0.72
Tools and hardware	53	6.45	0.92
Iron and steel products ..	34	4.14	0.60
Cotton goods	17	2.07	0.26
Wholesale trade	70	8.52	7.83
Retail trade	39	4.74	16.69
Wholesale and retail	35	4.26	5.91
Laundries	13	1.58	4.75

Source: Treasury Department and *Statistics of Income for 1937*.

industry comprised only 0.3 per cent of the total number of companies with net income in 1937, they represented 3.9 per cent of those with net income above $100,000 distributing less than 40 per cent of their income.

An unusual number of machine tool companies and manufacturers of other types of machinery are also found in the group distributing less than 40 per cent net income. They constituted 6.0 per cent of this group compared to 0.7 per cent of all companies with net income. Manufacturers of tools and hardware also made up 6.5 per cent of the former group compared with 0.9 per cent representation in all net income companies. The manufacture of machine tools, industrial machinery, etc., is subject to violent increases in investments in a period such as 1936-1937. Since they are also generally closely held corporations, the effects of the undistributed profits tax were unusually great.

On the other hand, a large proportion of the companies distributing less than 40 per cent of their earnings were in more stable industries such as wholesale and retail trade. All together 17.5 per cent of the companies in this category with incomes above $100,000 were trade corporations. However, considering their numerical importance in the entire business population, 30.4 per cent of all companies with net income in 1937, they are under-represented in the limited dividend group. Since their capital requirements are satisfied in large part by short-term bank loans needed to finance inventories of goods and accounts receivable, this is not surprising.

In general then, the evidence corroborates the view that companies requiring capital investment for expansion tended to plow back a larger proportion of their earnings for this purpose.[20] Either because of their lack of access to the capital markets or because of the nature of ownership, they were willing to pay a high price in terms of a surtax for this purpose.

20 Other industries distributing a relatively small part of profits in 1937 were: Agricultural machinery (44.2 per cent); airplanes (48.4 per cent); construction above ground (49.6 per cent); motion picture producers (54.8 per cent); other amusements (52.2 per cent). *Taxation of Corporate Enterprise*, T.N.E.C. Monograph No. 9, p. 179.

The compulsion to reinvest at the expense of the surtax is evidenced in many cases outside these particular fields. Douglas Aircraft, for example, experienced a three-fold expansion of its business in 1937 which necessitated a considerable increase in working capital and investment in tooling, plant, and other assets. The urgency of retaining over $1,000,000 of earnings in 1937 to finance these expenditures at an apparent sacrifice of $272,600 in surtaxes, is evidenced by the fact that its current liabilities expanded by almost $6,000,000 and its ratio of current assets to current liabilities (current ratio) was reduced by one half from 3.6 in 1936 to 1.8 in 1937. Net working capital which increased about $3,000,000 in 1936 as a result of new financing, was substantially reduced in 1937 as a result of its capital expenditures.

The Gillette Rubber Company paid a surtax of $108,000 in 1937 as a price for retention of over one-half million dollars in earnings. The use of these funds for expansion is evidenced by an increased investment in plant property and equipment of approximately the same amount retained. Two thirds of the common stock had been acquired indirectly by United States Rubber Company which also advanced funds to meet increased working capital requirements. While additional capital might have been acquired through advances from U. S. Rubber, or sale of stock, this would have represented an additional drain on U. S. Rubber which might not have been warranted under the circumstances.

ADEQUACY OF LIQUID FUNDS

The surplus account simply reflects the equity of the owners in the assets of the corporation but gives no evidence of the composition of the offsetting assets. While dividends in cash and other assets would generally be paid out of the net increment in assets of the corporation resulting from profit on operations (and not out of capital) these assets may not be in distributable form. The unavailability of cash (or its equivalent, investments in marketable securities), however, evidences the current decision of management to employ these funds for alternative purposes such as investment in increased inventories or accounts receivable, in expenditures for new plant or equipment and tooling, or even in research, development or advertising, whose expenditure is capitalized and written off to profit and loss over a period of years.[21] Funds may have also been applied to the repayment of debts, in accordance with an obligation of the corporation whose decision was made at some previous time; or to the retirement of preferred stock, or even common stock.

The availability of cash [22] at the end of the taxable year, therefore, reflects the decisions of management with respect to alternative uses of corporation funds. If corporations distributing less than 40 per cent of their earnings, for example, had relatively greater amounts of cash remaining than corporations distributing 100 per cent or more of earnings, there would be *prima facie* evidence of undue retention of profits for non-productive purposes.[23] The fact was, however, that the relative amount of liquid funds retained by corporations distributing less than 40 per cent of earnings was actually less than that remaining to corporations following a more liberal dividend policy.

Table No. 10 presents a comparison of the relative cash position of these two groups of corporations at the end of the taxable year. It is rather significant that the companies paying no surtax were in a much healthier cash position after distributing all their earnings than those which distributed relatively little. Using adjusted net income as a basis of comparison, it is

21 It should not be overlooked that funds are made available not only from net profit on operations but also from unexpended allowances for depreciation, depletion and bad debts.

22 " Cash " includes government bonds which are held as a liquid investment almost equivalent to cash.

23 Unless, of course, the funds were retained for future planned investment, repayment of debts or other essential reserves.

TABLE NO. 10

RELATIONSHIP OF CASH AND GOVERNMENT BONDS TO ADJUSTED NET INCOME
Maximum Surtax Corporations and No-Surtax Corporations, 1937

Income class ($1000)	Adjusted net income	Cash	Government bonds	Total	Ratio of total to adjusted net income
	(Millions of dollars)				
	Corporations paying maximum surtax rate				
$ 100- 250	67.6	60.8	10.4	71.2	1.05
250- 500	51.6	68.6	8.4	77.0	1.49
500-1,000	51.1	53.1	11.5	64.6	1.26
1,000-5,000	74.9	58.8	10.9	69.7	0.92
over 5,000	27.3	30.4	...	30.4	1.11
Total	273.4	271.6	41.3	312.9	1.14
	Corporations paying no surtax				
100- 250	239.3	281.4	147.9	429.3	1.79
250- 500	213.2	227.4	109.5	336.9	1.58
500-1,000	239.4	246.1	126.9	373.0	1.56
1,000-5,000	748.3	752.3	325.7	1,078.0	1.44
over 5,000	1,266.2	637.9	188.1	826.0	0.65
Total	2,706.4	2,145.1	898.1	3,043.2	1.12

Source: United States Treasury Department and *Statistics of Income for 1937*.

seen that for all net income classes but the very largest, the ratio of cash was greater for the latter than the former. While the average for all income classes was approximately the same, comparison by net income class discloses the undue influence of the largest class in depressing the ratio for the latter group. Exclusion of the highest income class leaves an average ratio of cash to adjusted net income of 1.15 for the low dividend group compared to 1.54 for the high dividend group. Variations are found among income classes which are particularly great for corporations earning between $100,000 and $250,000, where the respective ratios are 1.05 and 1.79. The least disparity is found in the next larger income class, leading one to believe that dividend policies were less influenced by consideration of capital requirements and other legitimate needs for this size corporation than for any other class.

Similar relationship is found in the percentage of cash and government bonds to total *assets* of these two groups of corporations. These percentages are summarized as follows:

Net income class ($1,000)	Per cent	
	Maximum surtax	No surtax
$ 250- 500	5.3	6.9
500-1,000	4.0	6.4
1,000-5,000	3.7	5.0
over 5,000	4.6 [24]	3.2

These data show that, in general, corporations with a conservative dividend policy were actually left with less cash in relationship to their total assets than companies with a liberal dividend policy. Those corporations which managed to avoid the surtax entirely thus appeared to have a greater redundancy of cash than those paying the maximum rate. Whether attributable to a superior credit position, better access to the capital market, or simply to less need for expansion in assets or replacement of property is not known. It may be inferred, however, that the purpose of avoiding personal income taxes played a subordinate rôle to the reinvestment of funds for expansion, repayment of debts, retirement of preferred stock and other normal purposes.

Such average comparisons, however, conceal the ability of individual companies to pay cash dividends. In this respect it is of some interest to determine the extent to which it might have been possible for corporations distributing less than 40 per cent of their earnings to have made a 100 per cent distribution with the cash remaining. However impracticable this might have been, it, nevertheless, provides a convenient criterion for separating the more liquid from less liquid corporations. In 1937 about 55 per cent of those corporations with net income in excess of $100,000 had sufficient cash and government

24 For three returns.

bonds on hand at the end of the year to cover a 100 per cent distribution; the remaining 45 per cent of the companies would have been unable to distribute all of their earnings. Relatively few, however, (perhaps 20 per cent) clearly appeared to have a redundancy of cash. In the absence of other relevant data it is impossible to determine whether the retention of earnings was justified or not for necessary business purposes. In any event the number of companies involved (sixty to seventy-five out of 310 with net incomes above $250,000) does not indicate any significant avoidance of personal income taxes by use of the corporation device.

INVENTORY PROFITS

The rising price level up to September, 1937 generated an inflation in book profits which was largely fictitious in character. The completion of sale at increasing prices left a "windfall" gain which in large part was automatically absorbed by the cost of replacing the goods sold. To the extent reinvestment of these earnings was essential to the maintenance of the same physical inventory of materials, the profits were essentially illusory. The realization of cash on the transaction was only a transitory phenomenon in the flow of corporation funds which left little or nothing additional in liquid form and available for distribution to shareholders.

Yet the Treasury Department did not recognize the realities of this situation at the time. Its regulations for the valuation of inventories insisted upon the conventional practice of valuation at cost or market, whichever lower, or at cost. As a result, many companies were placed at a serious disadvantage in escaping the impact of the undistributed profits tax by the distribution of profits which originated in price changes and could easily be wiped out by a price reverse. This was particularly true of those industries with a disproportionately large investment in raw stocks whose turnover was relatively slow and whose prices were sensitive to market changes. Perhaps the best example is found in the tanning industry where inventories normally account for 60 to 70 per cent of total assets and turnover is very slow because of the ageing process. Other examples are found in the lumber industry, in tobacco, non-ferrous metals, rubber and oils.[25]

The reluctance of directors to distribute inventory profits is understandable, if somewhat exaggerated. Unless the effect of price variations were eliminated, payment of dividends out of such taxable profits would be equivalent to a partial liquidation of the assets. A very large portion of the book earnings was represented by nothing more substantial than a price change in the book value of the assets. Disbursement of such income would, therefore, make it impossible to replace the physical quantities essential to preserving the capital of the business intact. Moreover, as was well recognized by spokesmen for these industries, the book profits attributable to a rising market price are almost inevitably succeeded by comparable losses with a reversal in prices. Failure to retain a substantial part of these "profits," therefore, would ultimately result in a dangerous loss of reserves needed to protect the company against offsetting " losses " in the future.[26]

25 An interesting evidence of this phenomenon is to be found in the case of the American Oak Leather Company during 1935. Between January and December, 1935 the average price of hides had increased approximately 30 per cent; coincident with this price increase the value of inventories rose from $2,451,166 to $3,233,933, or approximately 32 per cent. Statutory net income after taxes amounted to $400,000 of which $79,000 was distributed in dividends, leaving about $320,000 reinvested in the business. The management estimated that the real profit realized on operations during this period, after eliminating the effect of price changes, was only approximately $56,000, substantially less than that determined by conventional accounting concepts. Testimony of Will H. Mooney, President, American Oak Leather Company before the Committee on Ways and Means, *Hearings, Revenue Act of 1936*, p. 634.

26 The taxable profits of tanners were reported to be largely wiped out by the decline in the price of hides which accompanied the business recession of 1937. Statement of I. R. Glass, representing the Tanners Council of America, before the Committee on Ways and Means, *Hearings, Revenue Act of 1938*, p. 430.

An alternative to liquidation of inventories was the borrowing of funds to finance the increased cost of their replacement, and to carry book accounts. The dangers inherent in this policy are clearly evident, however, except for the financing of any net *increase* in the physical volume of inventory, above the normal level; subsequent inventory losses would impair the liquidity of the loan and possibly result in forced liquidation of assets to repay the obligation. As a last resort, the corporation could finance the payment of dividends by the issuance of new stock with the use of preemptive rights. This solution, however, would have capitalized business profits whose fictitious character was determined by the arbitrary concept of taxable income prescribed by the Treasury Department, and not necessarily by the accounting concepts of the corporation itself which generally took cognizance of the real situation.

There were two possible remedies for the inventory problem which was peculiar to the heavy inventory industries. One was the lengthening of the accounting period which would recognize the effect of fluctuating prices on inventory profits and losses over the period of a business cycle. The allowance for a carry-forward (or carry-back) of business losses against profits for three or four years would have greatly mitigated the severity of the tax on this type of business.

An alternative remedy, advocated by industry, was the adaptation of accounting principles to the realities of the business. This objective was finally achieved in 1938 with the authorization by the Bureau of Internal Revenue of the " LIFO " or " last-in, first-out" principle of valuation, based on the permanent investment concept of normal inventories, which minimized cyclical variations in inventory gains or losses due to price changes. Such practice had by then been universally accepted as good accounting theory in many of these industries for the corporation's own purposes.

CAPITAL GAINS AND LOSSES

In one other important respect the statutory net income which provided the basis of the surtax was at variance with accepted accounting practice. Deduction of capital losses, after subtracting the amount of net capital gain, was limited to $2,000. Despite the fact that the ability of a corporation to distribute its net income was impaired by the extent of the capital loss, it was denied credit for this loss in excess of $2,000. While this may have been an important factor which restricted dividends in many cases, the full extent of this limitation is not known. It is more likely that corporations were either deterred from taking such losses, or delayed their realization until a more favorable opportunity.

CHAPTER IV

THE IMPACT ON CORPORATION CREDIT

1. Contracts Restricting the Payment of Dividends

The dividend policy of management was rigidly circumscribed in many instances by prior commitments to creditors (and preferred stockholders) which had been agreed to as a condition of a loan (or sale of stock). These protective provisions, commonly found in bond indentures or contracts with banks, imposed a serious handicap on efforts to avoid the undistributed profits tax. This situation was recognized by Congress in the Revenue Act of 1936. Where such a contract had been entered into in good faith by a formal written agreement with creditors prior to May 1, 1936, relief was afforded by a special dividend credit equal to the amount of limitation on dividends.[1]

Dividend credit was allowed in the case of two different types of contract which restricted the distribution of net income. The first, and more important, related to the amount by which *dividends* were limited in the taxable year; the second type governed the disposition of *earnings* of the taxable year for retirement of debt. The dividend credit was limited to the amount actually so paid or irrevocably set aside. However, credit could be taken for only one such type of contract limitation.

PROHIBITION OF DIVIDEND PAYMENTS

The first type of restriction applied to specific contractual prohibitions against the payment of dividends out of current year's earnings. The provision was tightly drawn and rigidly administered by the Bureau of Internal Revenue. Such contracts (1) had to be in writing; (2) executed by the corporation before May 1, 1936; (3) expressly deal with the limitation of

1 *Revenue Act of 1936*, Section 26(c).

dividends; (4) of some definite or ascertainable amount. The provision was interpreted by the Treasury Department as a means of honoring the terms of contracts protecting creditors against disbursement of corporation funds. For this reason no credit was allowed if the terms of the contract did not preclude taxable stock dividends.[2] Dividends on one class of stock which were subject to the approval of another class were considered valid prohibitions if the required approval was not secured.[3]

Despite the contention of critics that the strict interpretation by the Treasury Department practically precluded relief under this section of the law,[4] many corporations obtained substantial benefits. Perhaps the largest credit, approximately $9,500,000, in 1937, was enjoyed by the Alleghany Corporation which was not permitted to pay dividends while its bond covenant was violated. The terms of the indenture under which the three issues of collateral trust bonds had been issued provided that unless the appraised value of the collateral was equal to 150 per cent of the face amount of the bonds outstanding, the income was to be impounded by the Trustee and the corporation could not declare any dividends on any issue of stock. On May 1, 1937, there was a substantial deficiency in the required ratio for the Twenty Year Collateral Trust Convertible 5% Bonds due in 1950.[5] While dividends on preferred stock had actually been earned throughout the depression, and in 1937 the common stock earned 67 cents per share, as of June 30, 1937 dividend arrears amounted to $33 per share on the cumulative preferred.[6] So long as the value of the collateral remained below

2 I.T. 3133. *Internal Revenue Bulletin, Cum. Bull., 1937-2.* U. S. Treasury Dept.

3 *Ibid.*, I.T. 3139.

4 See, for example, M. Slade Kendrick, *The Undistributed Profits Tax* (Washington: Brookings Institution, 1937), p. 53.

5 Securities and Exchange Commission, *Report on the Study and Investigation of the Work, Activities, Personnel and Functions of Protective and Reorganization Committees*, Part VII, p. 360.

6 *Ibid.*, p. 362.

the stipulated ratio for the collateral trust bonds, due 1950, the corporation was powerless to pay dividends. For this reason a plan of reorganization was proposed which would exchange these bonds for prior preferred stock and $200 in cash.

The U. S. Rubber Company had long-standing restrictions on dividends incorporated in its first and refunding mortgage indenture executed February 15, 1917.[7] As a result of the new revenue law this company temporarily suspended plans to refinance this debt which would have sacrificed a dividend credit of about $7,500,000 in 1937 alone. Other corporations such as the Oliver Farm Equipment Co. and York Ice Machinery Co. were obligated not to pay dividends so long as any notes or debentures were outstanding, resulting in a dividend credit of about $2,000,000 and $1,000,000, respectively, in 1937. Many companies had agreed not to distribute earnings as a condition of loans from Federal lending agencies such as the Reconstruction Finance Corporation and the Federal Reserve Banks. Among the latter was the E. G. Budd Manufacturing Company which had taxable profits in 1937 of close to $1,000,000.

Corporations such as the United Merchants and Manufacturers Corporation scaled dividend payments with the amount of funded debt outstanding, as a result of which this company was able to claim a credit of around $1,000,000 in 1937. The Continental Roll and Steel Foundry Company received a similar credit under its obligation not to pay cash dividends which would reduce the ratio of current assets to current liabilities below two to one, the conventional current ratio. The W. F. Hall Printing Company failed to live up to its agreement to retire bonds in the amount of $307,500 annually and was entitled to credit for dividends in the amount of around one million dollars for this neglect. Many other instances could be cited of substantial benefits realized despite the tightness of the law.

7 This and the following examples were derived from *Moody's Manual of Investments*.

DISPOSITION OF PROFITS IN TAXABLE YEAR

Corporations obligated to pay or set aside a portion of the year's earnings in discharge of a debt were entitled to credit for the amount so paid or irrevocably set aside. Like the previous provision, such contracts had to be negotiated in writing prior to May 1, 1936 and had to deal expressly with the disposition of earnings and profits.[8] No credit was allowed, therefore, for sinking fund or redemption provisions which were not based on earnings. Since most sinking fund payments call for a stated yearly amortization of the debt without reference to earnings, and repayment of most debt contracts is not contingent upon the realization of earnings, the relief was rather limited in application. Neither was recognition given to amounts required to be set aside for redemption of preferred stock since these payments did not involve the discharge of a debt. While many benefits were probably realized under this provision, a spot check of various known contracts did not disclose any applicable.

AMOUNT AND DISTRIBUTION OF CREDITS ALLOWED

It is estimated that credits of at least $130,000,000 in 1936 and $114,000,000 in 1937 were claimed for contracts restricting payment of dividends (see Table No. 11).[9] These amounted to 2.1 per cent and 1.8 per cent, respectively, of the total dividend credits claimed in these years. While it is likely that many of the claims were disallowed by the Bureau of Internal Revenue they were, nevertheless, rather substantial.

Corporations with the largest taxable income benefited less in proportion to the total dividend paid credit than those with lower income. In 1937 credits of over $40,000,000 were claimed by corporations with net income in excess of $1,000,000. While

8 Sec. 26(c).

9 Estimates are possible only for corporations paying no surtax. Since most credits were probably applicable to 100 per cent of earnings, these cases comprise substantially all of the aggregate amount claimed.

TABLE NO. 11

CONTRACTS RESTRICTING PAYMENT OF DIVIDENDS
AMOUNT AND DISTRIBUTION BY INCOME CLASS—1937
Thousands of Dollars

Income class	Contracts restricting payment of dividends [1]	Total dividend paid credit [2]	Per cent
Under $5	$ 1,867	$ 67,671	2.8%
5- 10	1,887	81,147	2.3
10- 25	5,652	202,872	2.8
25- 50	6,316	227,942	2.8
50- 100	12,846	282,518	4.5
100- 250	17,882	460,652	3.9
250- 500	17,615	408,799	4.3
500-1,000	8,981	469,825	1.9
1,000-5,000	14,780	1,481,892	1.0
5,000 & over	26,533	2,505,769	1.1
Total	114,360	6,189,088	1.8

[1] Source: U. S. Treasury Department. The amount of credit for contracts restricting payment of dividends was derived from the difference between dividends paid and adjusted net income for those corporations paying no surtax.

[2] Source: *Statistics of Income for 1937*, pp. 11, 14.

36 per cent of the total credits, they amounted to only 1.1 per cent of aggregate dividend paid credit of this income class. Apparently the medium size corporations with incomes ranging from $50,000 to $500,000 derived the greatest advantage from this special provision, with an average of over 4 per cent of total dividend credit. The lowest income group also gained a substantial benefit which averaged about 2.7 per cent of their total dividend credit.

Whether or not the corporation had a formal or tacit agreement to withhold distribution of earnings for the protection of creditors, the surtax on undistributed earnings could be justified as a compensatory tax in lieu of payment of personal income tax on dividends. While the incidence of the tax would have been distributed capriciously among the shareholders (as it is, indeed, by any tax on corporate income), without reference to individual ability to pay, it is questionable if any less equity would have been served than that resulting from some fortuitous arrangement with creditors in the past which relieved fortunate shareholders entirely from the incidence of the tax on their increased equity in the corporation. However, in view of the lack of the same opportunity enjoyed by shareholders of other corporations to minimize taxes by a distribution of earnings, it would have been only fair to exact a compromise rate of say one half the maximum surtax of 20.5 per cent.

2. Statutory Limitations on Dividends

The laws of most states prohibit the payment of dividends when the capital of a corporation is impaired.[10] With few important exceptions an accumulated deficit must be made good before dividends may legally be declared.[11] The Treasury Department, however, did not recognize the validity of the corporate charter as a written contract restricting the payment of dividends. This position was supported by the apparent intent of the Congress in the enactment of the Revenue Act of 1936. The original House bill contained a provision relieving corporations so affected from payment of the surtax and substituted a flat tax instead, but this provision was struck out by the Senate and not restored in conference.[12] The conflict with state law was finally resolved in favor of the Federal government by a decision of the Supreme Court in 1940.[13] The defendant's case was based upon the charter provision which required it to

10 An excellent summary of these provisions is found in James C. Bonbright, *The Valuation of Property* (New York: McGraw-Hill & Co., 1937), Ch. XXVII. This is based on a series of articles published in the *Columbia Law Review* by Joseph L. Weiner and James C. Bonbright, Vols. 28 (1046); 29 (461); 30 (330, 954).

11 Important exceptions are found in the States of California, Delaware and Minnesota which permit the payment of dividends out of current net income, with certain limitations, even though the legal capital is impaired. Raymond P. Marple, *Capital Surplus and Corporate Net Worth* (New York: The Ronald Press, 1936), pp. 78-80.

12 *Revenue Bill of 1936*, H. R. 12395.

13 *Helvering v. Northwest Rolling Mills, Inc.*, 61 Supreme Court 109, Nov. 12, 1940.

conform to the laws of the State of Washington but the Court declared that, ". . . . what prohibited respondent from distributing dividends was not the provision of an executed written contract expressly dealing with the payment of dividends . . . . but a valid law of the State of Washington."

A considerable number of corporations were confronted with the problem of avoiding the maximum surtax without running afoul of the state law governing the distribution of dividends. Because of the possible liabilities incurred by directors for violations, they sought a way out of the dilemma by legal means. Fortunately for their purposes, this could be accomplished in most states with little difficulty by writing down the value of the stated capital; the accumulated deficit could then be charged against the capital surplus so created and dividends made technically possible out of current income. While the consent of the state is essential to a reduction in the par value of capital stock or a change in stated value, this is ordinarily accomplished more or less automatically when authorized by the stockholders of the corporation.[14] Some limitations are imposed by the laws of a few states but in the words of one authority, " . . . this opportunity, which is accompanied by no adequate safeguards on behalf of creditors and preferred stockholders, comes close to making a farce of American dividend law." [15]

No data are available on the number of corporations forced to eliminate an accumulated deficit as a prerequisite to dividend payments. Many instances may be cited, however, which attest the efficacy of this plan. The Yellow Truck and Coach Manufacturing Co., for example, carried out a major plan of recapitalization in 1936 for the purpose of eliminating a large deficit which precluded the payment of dividends.[16] As a result of

14 See Raymond P. Marple, *op. cit.*, pp. 97-101.

15 Bonbright, *op. cit.*, p. 914.

16 *Commercial and Financial Chronicle*, Vol. 143, p. 2388.

writing down the par value of common stock from $10 to $1 and retiring preferred stock held in the treasury, the capital was reduced from $30,000,000 to $19,498,000 and the deficit was wiped out with the resulting capital surplus. The company was then able to proceed with an ambitious plan of financing the payment of dividends through an issue of stock rights, a large part of the funds being supplied by General Motors Corporation, the principal owner of its preferred and common stock.

The presence of an accumulated deficit of $826,605 barred the way to payment of dividends by the Marchant Calculating Machine Co. Reduction in the par value of its common stock from $10 to $5 created a capital surplus of $1,000,000 against which this was written off and made possible the distribution of $541,600 out of earnings of $644,000 in 1936.[17] Athey Truss Wheel Co. also facilitated the payment of $149,000 in dividends out of net earnings of $200,000 in 1936 by eliminating a book deficit of $100,000 through the reduction in par value of its common stock from $5 to $4. The United Paperboard Company eliminated a large deficit of over $9,000,000 by writing down the par value of its common stock from $12,000,000 to $2,400,000. The corporation accomplished this by reducing the par value from $100 to $10 and exchanging two shares of new stock for one of old.

However, not all such plans were successful. An interesting case of the failure of the stockholders to ratify a proposed plan of recapitalization is presented by the B. B. & R. Knight Corporation, textile manufacturers. The president proposed a reorganization plan to eliminate a book deficit of $6,000,000 by writing down the value of capital stock from $8,000,000 to $1,500,000.[18] Despite the announced purpose of this plan to enable the distribution of dividends which would avoid the undistributed profits tax, the stockholders failed to approve it,

17 *Moody's Manual of Investments*, 1937.

18 *Commercial and Financial Chronicle*, Vol. 143, p. 2683.

and the corporation was subject to a surtax of $46,000 on net profits of $210,600 in 1936.[19]

The relative ease with which the legal capital of a corporation may be altered at the will of the stockholders raises a serious question of proper business conduct which is not easily answered. In principle, the legal capital of a corporation is presumed to constitute a so-called "trust fund" for the protection of creditors, and in many cases preferred stockholders. Because of the limited liability enjoyed by a corporation, any arbitrary reduction in this legal capital would appear to jeopardize the interests of those parties who relied on this protection in financing the requirements of the business. The distribution of corporate funds to stockholders should, therefore, be limited to such increment in the net assets of a business which would leave the original contribution of this capital fund unimpaired. Any other policy would constitute a distribution of capital.

On the other hand, the revaluation of the legal capital of a corporation is frequently a formal acknowledgment of a practical situation which is beyond repair. It reflects a long process of deterioration in the assets of a business by the liquidation of inventories, loss in value or abandonment of plant and equipment, which has resulted from the vicissitudes of a business cycle or secular change in demand for the product. Frequently, as in the case of public utilities, it is occasioned by the write-down of inflated plant valuations arising at the time of acquisition of the properties. Just as an expanding business may capitalize a permanent increase in the net worth of the corporation by stock dividends, or through merger or consolidation, so a declining business may scale down its capital to a more permanent value consistent with the contracted level of operations. Such revaluations are sanctioned by statutory law and, while subject to abuse, cannot be undertaken recklessly without exposing the corporation to possible unfavorable reaction on its future credit.

19 *Moody's Manual of Investments*, 1937.

While the conflict between state laws governing the payment of dividends and the Federal surtax on undistributed profits was the subject of much righteous indignation, relatively few corporations whose legal capital was impaired appeared to suffer disability in the payment of dividends. Analysis of 240 large corporations paying no dividends in 1937 disclosed that only 65, or 27 per cent, had book deficits. All together it is estimated that not more than 375 corporations with accumulated deficits in this year failed to pay dividends. Whether the presence of the book deficit was the proximate reason for the failure to distribute earnings is not known, but even assuming dividends were technically impossible for this reason, the small number of cases does not evidence any widespread hardship under the law. Neither was every corporation with an accumulated deficit precluded thereby from the payment of dividends, since a far greater number of corporations reporting book deficits made distribution of the earnings of the year.

Statutory laws restricting the payment of dividends thus presented less of an obstacle to the avoidance of the Federal undistributed profits tax than is commonly believed. Even allowing for variations in the determination of net profits for tax purposes and for private purposes, it was possible for a great number of companies to pay dividends even though their capital was impaired; and those which were faced with technical obstacles were able to eliminate them with little difficulty.

What may have been expedient for tax purposes, however, was not necessarily conducive to sound financial policy which frowns on the payment of dividends out of capital, however sanctioned or facilitated by law. The Federal government not only arbitrarily narrowed its focus on the net income derived in the period of one year, thus reversing a trend in the opposite direction of permitting a two year carry-forward of losses, but also encouraged the distribution of a single year's income without reference to its flow in time. While the elimination of an accumulated deficit may be justified in many cases, and might have been undertaken in the absence of the surtax, this practice was accelerated with possible undesirable effects. Where more prudent judgment might have dictated the conservation of capital, management was frequently swayed by the relative tax advantage of effecting a distribution of earnings. Where payment of dividends out of current earnings was possible even when capital was impaired, the sound principle of maintaining the capital intact was overridden by the expediency of shifting the impact of the tax to the stockholders directly, for the purpose of minimizing its burden. The Federal government, through its compulsion on the payment of dividends, thus clearly promoted objectionable financing practices whose reform was overdue.

How this situation might have been avoided without incurring other abuses or injustices is difficult to say. The original bill provided exemption to those corporations whose capital was impaired. Equally serious inequities might have been created by such blanket relief since many corporations would have continued to shelter themselves behind an accumulated technical deficit whose correction was realistically overdue. Perhaps the middle course of permitting a carry-back of profits against losses for a reasonable number of years would have been the most realistic approach. In this way an opportunity would have been provided of restoring a part, at least, of the unusual losses of the depression that contributed so much to the seriousness of the situation at the time.

3. Insolvent Corporations

Exemption from the surtax was provided for corporations in receivership or bankruptcy.[20] Many corporations technically insolvent had been placed in the hands of a receiver in equity or trustee in bankruptcy as a result of the drastic deflation of the depression in the early thirties. Amendments to the Bankruptcy Act in 1933 through Section 77, dealing with

20 *Revenue Act of 1936*, Sec. 14(d).

railroads, and Section 77B, dealing with public utilities and industrials, expedited the reorganization of corporations in default and encouraged the employment of this technique for readjustment of their capital structure. Pending reorganization and discharge from the court, they could continue to enjoy the protection of the tax law against distribution of substantial earnings which in many cases accompanied the business recovery of 1935-1937. Encouragement was, therefore, given not only to the adoption of this technique for the settlement of claims but also to the prolongation of the process which was lengthy and costly at best under normal conditions.

Comparable relief, however, was not afforded corporations whose reorganization was undertaken privately outside the jurisdiction of the courts. Such extra-legal adjustments of liabilities are commonly undertaken through *extension agreements* whereby the management of the corporation is placed under the supervision of its principal creditors and an equitable adjustment of its debts arrived at without jeopardizing the continuation of the business. The management committee appointed by the creditors is frequently given voting control of the capital stock with power to apply the earnings of the business against their claims. To all intents and purposes, this control is equivalent to the power of a receiver or trustee in bankruptcy, but rests on voluntary consent of the parties rather than the sanction of law. A complete moratorium is given to payment of corporate debt, the final settlement of which is deferred over a period of time but seldom in the hope of realizing 100 cents on the dollar. In this way the uncertainty, cost, stigma of receivership, and possible liquidation in bankruptcy are avoided in the hope of salvaging a going concern and expectation of future business.

Not only are dividend payments inconsistent with the rehabilitation of the business but are frequently prohibited by the creditors. Specific prohibitions on the payment of dividends originating prior to May, 1936 provided a measure of relief, but such formal agreements were by no means universal; and there is evidence of many corporations laboring under an old indebtedness which were unable to employ their increased earnings of 1936-1937 to improve their credit position without incurring a large additional tax on undistributed profits.[21] Moreover, those companies which submitted to voluntary reorganization and common law composition of their debts after the effective date were denied the same measure of relief from taxes to which they would have been entitled under the alternatives of receivership or bankruptcy. The premium placed on judicial reorganization thus discouraged the use of extension agreements which provided a definitely superior method of adjustment in cases of small and medium size corporations whose capital structure was simple and creditors few.

4. Effect on Corporation Credit

The maintenance of corporate credit is vitally affected by the prudence with which corporate management disposes of its earnings and profits. The apparent conflict of the undistributed profits tax with the preservation of sound credit policies is one of those intangible effects of the law on the expansion of business which it is impossible to measure statistically. Not only is the further extension of business credit frequently conditioned upon the agreement of the corporation to conserve its funds for the protection of creditors (as exemplified by contracts restricting payment of dividends) but the adequacy of the working capital is a critical factor in the future extension of credit to a business. This concept has been embodied in the current ratio which has been established at a conventional standard of current assets to liabilities of two to one. Banks and trade creditors as well as professional credit analysts viewed with some misgivings the emphasis of the tax law on

21 See brief filed with the Committee on Ways and Means by the National Association of Credit Men, *Hearings*, Revenue Act of 1938, pp. 564-65.

the attenuation of a corporation's working capital position.[22] The degree with which dividend payments are scrutinized by banks is all too well known by those who have ever applied for a line of credit.[23]

There is some evidence that the distribution of earnings was influenced by the burden of corporation debt. Analysis was made by the T.N.E.C. of the magnitude of the surtax (as a percentage of net income before interest charges) paid by corporations with different equity ratios.[24] In 1937 a sample of 609 manufacturing and trade corporations showed the following relationship of the undistributed profits tax (as a percentage of net income before interest charges) to the various equity ratio classes:[25]

Equity ratio class	Surtax percentage
Under 2	2.8
2 to 4	2.2
4 to 8	2.3
8 to 12	1.2
12 to 16	1.1
16 to 20	0.8
Over 20	0.2

It seems clear from these data that corporations with the largest proportion of debt (those with the lowest equity ratio) paid the heaviest undistributed profits tax. Those whose capital was supplied primarily on an ownership basis (with the

22 Testimony of the National Association of Credit Men, *ibid.*, pp. 565-66.

23 A concrete example is provided by the testimony of the B. F. Sturtevant Co., which had contracted with the Federal Reserve Bank of Boston for a five year term loan. When approached by the management on the question of distribution to avoid surtaxes, the Bank characteristically refused permission. Because of the Bank's power to call the loan if it believed dividends unjustified, the corporation naturally refrained from distribution. *Ibid.*, p. 573.

24 Clifford L. Hynning, *Taxation of Corporate Enterprise*, T.N.E.C. Monograph No. 9 (Washington, 1941), pp. 94-95. The equity ratio is the ratio of corporation net worth to total debt, including long term debt and current liabilities.

25 *Ibid.*, p. 185.

highest equity ratios) paid the lightest surtaxes. A similar pattern is shown by corporations of the same asset size, except for the smallest size classes. In other words, the percentage of earnings distributed tended to vary directly with the relative freedom from corporation debt.

There are notable exceptions, however, to the generalization that the undistributed profits tax was heaviest on "debt ridden" corporations. The amount of surtaxes paid in 1936 by this same group of companies does not show any relationship to the size of the equity ratio.[26] Neither does there appear to be any relationship in 1937 for particular industry groups such as building products, paper and transportation equipment. Unfortunately, the data do not include public utilities and railroads where the proportion of debt is unusually large. It may reasonably be concluded, however, that the undistributed profits tax tended to discourage creditor financing.

On the other hand, reasonable distribution of earnings is not necessarily incompatible with the maintenance of corporate credit. Short term credit, in particular, serves a continuing function in financing the working capital requirements of American business. Liquidation of loans, when they are paid off, is ordinarily accomplished by liquidation of the current assets for which the funds were originally required, rather than from the profit itself realized on their sale. While the retention of earnings increases the equity of the creditor and strengthens the credit of the borrower, it is fallacious to believe that the choice always lies between the payment of dividends and the repayment of the loan. To have permitted a dividend credit for repayment of loans, as argued by some, would have taken a rather naive view of business finance and defeated the purpose of the surtax itself.

Where the purpose of the loan was to finance permanent investment in working capital or fixed plant, its repayment out of the net profits of the business enhances the equity of

26 *Idem.*

stockholders no less than the current reinvestment of earnings for the same purpose. Use of borrowed funds simply enables the corporation to anticipate the investment of its own capital, which in effect replaces the borrowed capital concurrently with the repayment of the debt. In principle, therefore, a corporation has no less *ability to pay* if its earnings are committed to the fulfillment of an obligation than if the funds were reinvested in the business in the first instance. In the former case, the interests of the creditors might be sacrificed (and perhaps the corporate credit); in the latter case, the prospective expansion of the business would be curtailed by the amount of the tax.

The impact of the surtax on debt-burdened corporations could have been alleviated somewhat by the allowance of a dividend credit for bond interest payments. For this purpose adjusted net income would be taken *before* deduction of bond interest and credit given for interest payments as a means of reducing the surtax rate applicable to the balance remaining undistributed.[27] The employment of funded debt rather than equity securities may be dictated by financial exigencies or by the feasibility of "trading on the equity." (One factor influencing the use of bonds is the deduction allowed for bond interest under the normal corporation tax itself.) Since bond interest is an alternative contractual form of distributing the earnings of a business, allowance of a credit for its payment would have not only recognized the realities of corporation finance but also would have given relief to many areas of hardship such as the railroad industry. No purpose would have been served, of course, in forcing a distribution of earnings.

27 For example, a corporation with net income of $1,000,000 after deduction of normal taxes but before interest payments of $600,000 would be credited with a distribution of 60 per cent of its earnings. The surtax on the balance would be only $53,000 instead of $82,000 paid under the graduated rates.

CHAPTER V

TAX AVOIDANCE BY USE OF NON-CASH DIVIDENDS

1. General

CREDIT was allowed only for dividends legally subject to the personal income tax. Congress accordingly encouraged the payment of non-cash dividends by expressly authorizing credit for dividends paid in kind, in obligations, and in stock or stock rights, subject, however, to constitutional limitations on the concept of taxable income.[1] As a result, many unusual practices which left their mark on the corporate financial structure were availed of for the purpose of tax avoidance.

While the proliferation of dividends took many forms, the cash dividend maintained its predominant role: In 1936, 94.4 per cent of all taxable dividends were in this form.[2] Their importance varied, however, with the size of corporation net income, ranging from 87.3 per cent for the $10,000-$25,000 net income class to 97.8 per cent for the largest income class with over $5,000,000 net income. In this respect there appear to be three distinct income groups of corporations, with the following approximate proportions of non-cash dividends:

Net income	Per cent
Below $100,000	12
$100,000-5,000,000	7
Over $5,000,000	2

The most important form of non-cash dividend was in assets of the corporation, other than cash, amounting to 2.7 per cent of taxable dividends in 1936. Obligations of the company, in the form of scrip, notes and bonds represented 2.2 per cent of

1 *Revenue Act of 1936*, Sec. 27(a), (c), (d), (e).

2 See Table No. 13, *infra*, p. 104 for the following data.

the total, and stock dividends, the least important, with only 0.75 per cent of total taxable distributions. The relative importance, implication and limitations of these principal classes of taxable dividends are discussed below.

2. Stock Dividends

The Revenue Act of 1936 expressly provided credit for taxable dividends paid in the corporation's own stock.[3] The question of taxability, however, was one that had beset tax administration for years and still remained unsettled at the time of the Act. What might otherwise have proved a clear avenue for tax avoidance was thus blocked by the uncertainty of whether the particular type of stock dividend constituted taxable income in the eyes of the Supreme Court.

Twenty years previous stock dividends were made taxable "to the amount of their cash value" by the Revenue Act of 1916. Only four years later the Supreme Court declared that such dividends did not constitute income under the provisions of the 16th Amendment.[4] However, this case was limited to a determination of the taxability of common stock dividends paid to common shareholders. Since the decision turned on the issue of whether the proportionate interest of the shareholders in the corporation was altered by the distribution, the question still remained whether other types of dividends represented taxable income. It was not until 1936, the first year of the undistributed profits tax, that the court clarified its concept of taxable income to include common dividends paid on preferred stock.[5]

The taxability of preferred dividends paid on common stock still remained to be settled. While it seemed clear from the Koshland decision that such dividends were taxable where both

3 Sec. 115 (a), (f).

4 *Eisner* v. *Macomber*, 252 U. S. 189 (1920).

5 *Koshland* v. *Helvering*, 297 U. S. 702 (1936).

issues were previously outstanding,[6] it was debatable whether the issuance of preferred stock to common stockholders was taxable if only common was outstanding. Despite an adverse decision in a lower court,[7] the Treasury Department held that such dividends did constitute income within the meaning of the 16th Amendment. Consequently, the issue was still in doubt at the time of the undistributed profits tax as to whether preferred dividends paid on common stock were taxable under all circumstances. This question was not resolved until 1943 when the Supreme Court decided that where only common stock was outstanding a new issue of preferred to common stockholders did not represent income since the proportionate interest of the owners of the corporation was undisturbed.[8]

In order to circumvent the limitations of the courts on the taxability of stock dividends, the Congress enunciated a new principle, that of optional stock dividends. The Revenue Act of 1936 provided that a dividend was taxable if declared payable in either stock (or stock rights) or in money (or property) at the election of the stockholder. The legality of such optional dividends received in stock was, of course, still subject to the interpretation of the Supreme Court.

In 1936 there was a substantial increase in the amount of stock dividends; they declined to about half the 1936 amount in 1937. Compared with the previous and following years, it would appear that the surtax had given an impetus to this opportunity for avoidance. The record for all corporations earning net income is presented as follows:

6 See e.g., *Helvering* v. *Gowran*, 302 U. S. 238. This case, decided December 6, 1937 on another issue declared, "This preferred stock had substantially the same attributes as that involved in the Koshland case."

7 *Torrens* v. *Commissioner*, 31 B.T.A. 787 (1934).

8 *Strassburger* v. *Commissioner*, 318 U. S. 604, April 5, 1943. In this case all the common stock was owned by one person.

Year	Stock dividends ($1,000)
1933	$ 80,450
1934	173,419
1935	112,162
1936	335,319
1937	170,945
1938	76,146
1939	87,202

Source: *Statistics of Income for 1941*, p. 270.

Further analysis of the data, however, discloses that only a small fraction of these dividends were taxable. Table No. 12 presents a breakdown of stock dividends paid out by corporations subject to the tax in 1936, the biggest year. Out of $287,600,000 stock dividends paid by these corporations[9] only $49,600,000 or 16.2 per cent were taxable. In 1937, taxable stock dividends increased to $60,400,000 despite a decline in the total amount of stock dividends to $162,800,000 for corporations subject to the surtax. The percentage of taxable dividends to the total was, therefore, 37.1 per cent.

The most important form of taxable dividend in 1936 was the issuance of preferred stock to common stockholders. These dividends aggregated $24,148,000, about one-half of the total. No dividend credit was taken, however, for about 30 per cent of the preferred stock distributed on common, presumably because preferred stock was not previously outstanding. These issues may have been made in anticipation of further distribution in future years as a means of tax avoidance.

Preferred stock distributions to preferred shareholders comprised about 10 per cent of the total taxable stock dividends. Common stock dividends to preferred stockholders made up an additional 11 per cent. The second largest category, however, evidenced the successful distribution of common stock under

9 Discrepancy with the figure of $335,300,000 listed above may be accounted for by stock dividends of corporations exempt from the tax, including banks.

TABLE NO. 12

TYPES OF DIVIDENDS PAID—1936

CORPORATIONS SUBJECT TO SURTAX ON UNDISTRIBUTED PROFITS

(Thousands of dollars)

Types of dividend	Taxable	Non-taxable	Total
Cash	$6,178,019	......	$6,178,019
Treasury stock	6,367	......	6,367
Other assets	149,524	......	149,524
Obligations of the corporation	144,203	......	144,203
Common on preferred	5,601	$ 433	6,034
Preferred on preferred	5,065	2,200	7,265
Preferred on common	24,148	10,021	34,169
Common on common	2,009	225,471	227,480
Optional mode of payment			
Cash	13,886	......	13,886
Common Stock	12,739	......	12,739
Other	18,882	......	18,882
Total	$6,560,443	$238,125	$6,798,568
Recapitulation			
Cash	$6,191,905	......	$6,191,905
Other assets (incl. Treasury Stock)	174,773	......	174,773
Obligations	144,203	......	144,203
Stock	49,562	238,125	287,687
Total	$6,560,443	$238,125	$6,798,568

Source: Treasury Department; *Bulletin of the Treasury Department*, February, 1940.

the newly authorized optional mode of payment. All together $12,739,000 of taxable stock dividends were distributed under this plan, about 25 per cent of the total.[10] Credit was also claimed for about $2,000,000 of common stock dividends issued to common stockholders.[11]

10 For a thorough analysis of the employment of optional stock dividends see David L. Rolbein, "Non-Cash Dividends and Stock Rights as Methods for Avoidance of the Undistributed Profits Tax," *The Journal of Business of the University of Chicago*, Vol. XII, No. 3, July, 1939, pp. 221-264.

11 In 1936 the income tax form provided for the entry of taxable common stock dividends on common stock, but in 1937 no similar space was provided. Possibly the amount claimed in 1936 represented different issues of common stock classified with respect to voting privileges. Such classification raises an interesting question of taxability which was subsequently decided in the negative by the Supreme Court. *Helvering* v. *Sprouse* in a joint decision with *Strassburger* v. *Helvering*, 318 U. S., 604 (1943). The Court

The largest class of non-taxable dividends is found, as expected, in the case of common stock distribution to common shareholders. Apparently the same factors continued to operate in 1936 on an accelerated scale with respect to the capitalization of earned surplus, long since determined by the Supreme Court to be non-taxable. It is difficult to account for the decline in common stock dividends in 1937 except possibly by the business recession which set in toward the end of the year.

Taxable stock dividends represented less than one per cent of total dividends distributed by corporations subject to the undistributed profits tax in each year. (The exact percentages were 0.75 in 1936 and 0.85 in 1937). Some variation with the size of the corporation is apparent from the accompanying Table No. 13 but this was not significant for companies below $1,000,000 income where the amount ranged from 1.0 to 1.5 per cent of total dividends. The largest corporations made relatively less use of non-cash dividends, with taxable stock dividends of corporations earning over $5,000,000 amounting to only 0.4 of one percent of total dividends. A similar pattern is evident in 1937, except that smaller companies with income below $25,000 made proportionately less use of stock dividends than the medium size corporations.

The most striking evidence of the unpopularity of stock dividends is provided by the small number of corporations which took advantage of this opportunity for tax avoidance. Out of 181,194 companies subject to the surtax in 1937, only 648 companies issued taxable stock dividends—about one-third of one per cent. Similar data for previous years are not available. One thorough analysis of stock dividends, however, leads to the conclusion that, with few exceptions, such

---

ruled that the issuance of non-voting common to voting common shareholders did not alter their voice in the corporation or their participation in profits or assets, in liquidation.

distributions resulted directly from the undistributed profits tax.[12]

TABLE NO. 13

TYPES OF TAXABLE DIVIDENDS AND THEIR DISTRIBUTION BY INCOME CLASS, 1936

Net income class ($1,000)	Total taxable distributions	Cash	Stock	Obligations of the corporation	Other assets [1]
		Amount (millions of dollars)			
Under $5 ...	$ 75.2	$ 67.0	$ 1.1	$ 3.5	$ 3.6
5- 10 ...	77.9	68.9	1.0	4.0	4.0
10- 25 ...	206.5	180.3	2.7	12.7	10.9
25- 50 ...	244.0	213.5	2.8	15.6	12.1
50- 100 ...	302.1	270.5	3.0	14.5	14.1
100- 250 ...	487.4	452.6	5.3	17.6	11.9
250- 500 ...	444.1	413.9	6.5	10.7	12.9
500-1,000 ...	544.8	511.3	5.5	16.2	11.8
1,000-5,000 ...	1,487.2	1,391.0	9.9	47.1	39.2
Over 5,000 ...	2,681.1	2,622.9	11.6	2.2	54.3
Total ...	6,560.4	6,191.9	49.6	144.2	174.8
		Percentage of total taxable dividends			
Under $5 ...	100%	89.0%	1.5%	4.7%	4.8%
5- 10 ...	100	88.4	1.3	5.1	5.1
10- 25 ...	100	87.3	1.3	6.2	5.3
25- 50 ...	100	87.5	1.2	6.4	5.0
50- 100 ...	100	89.5	1.0	4.8	4.7
100- 250 ...	100	92.9	1.1	3.6	2.4
250- 500 ...	100	93.2	1.5	2.4	2.9
500-1,000 ...	100	93.9	1.0	3.0	2.2
1,000-5,000 ...	100	93.5	0.7	3.2	2.6
Over 5,000 ...	100	97.8	0.4	0.1	2.0
Total ...	100	94.4	0.75	2.2	2.7

Source: Treasury Department.

[1] Includes Treasury Stock and Investments.

Failure to exploit the stock dividend method of tax avoidance more fully may be attributed to many different factors. Perhaps the most important deterrent was the uncertainty regarding their taxability. Where the specific issue had not been decided by the Supreme Court, corporations were reluctant to run the risk of a possible nullification which might

12 David L. Rolbein, *op. cit.*, pp. 233-240.

subject them to a contingent liability for surtaxes at an indefinite time in the future.[13]

Where stock dividends clearly represented taxable income the capital structure of many corporations circumscribed their utilization for this purpose. It was inferred from the Koshland decision handed down in 1936 that a necessary condition of the taxability of preferred dividends to common stockholders was the prior existence of preferred stock. (This was affirmed in 1943, as explained above.) Since the capitalization of small corporations is limited primarily to capital or common stock the opportunity for tax avoidance was effectively precluded in the great majority of cases.[14] The opportunity for paying common dividends to preferred stockholders was likewise precluded. Moreover, preferred dividends are ordinarily payable only in cash; unless the consent of the shareholders to a common dividend could be secured, management was powerless to use this avenue of escape. Except in the case of accumulated arrears and complete recapitalization such consent is usually difficult to secure.[15] These conditions probably account for the fact that both common and preferred stock dividend payments to preferred stockholders were relatively unimportant and amounted to only 11 per cent and 10 per cent, respectively, of the total taxable stock distributions.

13 This risk is evidenced by the position of the Treasury Department with respect to the treatment of such dividends: "In any case in which the taxability of the distribution in the hands of the shareholders is debatable, it will be general policy of the Bureau to allow tentatively a dividend paid credit in an amount equal to the fair market value of the stock distributed, provided the corporation claiming the credit, upon request by the Bureau, files with the Commissioner the proper waivers of agreement to protect the interests of the government pending the final determination of the taxability to the shareholders of the distribution . . ." I.T. 3037 *Cum. Bul.*, 1937-1, p. 90.

14 Of 381 small corporations analyzed by C. L. Merwin, Jr., only 49, or 12.8 per cent had preferred stock in 1936. T.N.E.C. Monograph No. 15, Appendix F, Tables I-A to I-E.

15 One such case was that of the Cooper-Bessemer Corp., Rolbein, *op. cit.*, p. 231.

Another factor which militated against the use of stock dividends was the reluctance to complicate the capital structure of the corporation by the use of different classes of stock. Successive issues, moreover, would tend to distort the capital structures, particularly if preferred stock were employed. The nuisance of handling fractional shares presented another obstacle. Technical problems were also involved in securing the necessary consent of shareholders, filing amendments to the charter and other legal matters connected with their issue.

Another limitation was the problem of arriving at a market price for purpose of establishing a fair value for the stock. Since relatively few corporations are listed or traded on an organized exchange, there was little opportunity to establish a fair value of stock for the vast majority of corporations. While the optional stock dividend presented a way out, corporations ran the risk of a choice of cash. Associated with this lack of market was the inability of stockholders to sell their stock dividends where necessary in order to pay the income tax thereon.

3. Obligations of the Corporations

Of considerably greater importance than stock dividends was the employment of the corporations' own obligations in the payment of dividends. These distributions amounted to about $144,000,000 in 1936 and represented 2.2 per cent of total dividend payments. The greatest use of this expedient was made by small and medium size corporations. Corporations with net income below $100,000 issued obligations equal to 5.5 per cent of all taxable dividend payments, compared to 3.1 per cent for companies with net income between $100,000 and $5,000,000, and only 0.1 per cent of dividend payments of those with income in excess of $5,000,000.

These obligations assumed many forms. They ranged from dividend script which deferred the cash payment until the following year, to long term liabilities such as the 15 year 3½ per cent debenture of the Reynolds Metal Co. The majority varied in maturity from three to ten years—a rather long time to postpone dividends.[16] In order to command a market value for income tax purposes all obligations were interest bearing with rates ranging from the 2 per cent convertible debenture of the Parker-Wolverine Co. to the highest rate noted of 8 per cent on the capital notes of the Lane Co.

The payment of dividends in notes and bonds of the corporation effectively avoided the surtax without an immediate drain on corporate funds. The day of reckoning was simply postponed, however, and not necessarily avoided. It is questionable, therefore, how far this practice could be carried by a corporation without accumulating an undue burden of debt which might ultimately impair the value of the common stock—on which virtually all these payments were made. In principle, the continued payment of interest charges on such an accumulated debt would be at the expense of dividend payments. In this way, dividends would, in effect, be converted to a fixed charge for which a credit was allowed in the determination of taxable income. To the extent that the obligations were retained by the stockholders, interest would be received in lieu of dividends, and little danger would be incurred by the corporation for default of such interest or payment of the obligation at maturity —since the creditors would also be the owners of the corporation.

On the other hand, the stockholders were faced with the problem of discharging their tax liabilities on the taxable dividend received. It is likely that many were forced to liquidate their notes to secure the necessary funds (or to borrow on the notes as collateral). In this respect, there may have been a tendency for their ownership to be dissociated from the common stockholders and for the development of a conflict of interest between the two parties. This problem was avoided in many instances by supplementary cash distributions which

16 See Rolbein, *op. cit.*, pp. 244-45.

provided the means of discharging personal tax liabilities on the obligation.[17]

While many companies employed such obligations in both years,[18] the surtax was repealed and the practice was never carried to its ultimate conclusion. It is likely that such dividends were encouraged largely in the expectation that the undistributed profits tax would be repealed sooner or later, and that no serious consequences would, therefore, develop. While those companies which adopted this policy do not appear to have suffered any ill effects, the influence of an undistributed profits tax in this respect does not appear to be conducive to a healthy corporate structure.

4. Other Assets

Dividends paid in assets of the corporation other than cash represented the largest single category of non-cash dividends. The total credit claimed in 1936 amounted to about $175,000,000, or 2.7 per cent of total taxable disbursements. Again, this type of dividend met greater favor with the smaller companies, as measured by net income, but less variation was found among income groups than in the case of stock dividends and dividends paid in obligations. About 5.0 per cent of the distributions of corporations with income below $100,000 were in this form—twice the proportion (2.5 per cent) employed by corporations with income between $100,000 and $5,000,000. Corporations in the largest income class, with income above $5,000,000, made considerably greater use of this opportunity for tax avoidance than other forms of non-cash dividends, paying out $54,300,000 in value of "other assets," or 30 per cent of the total. These represented about 2.0 per cent of their total taxable dividends, and accounted for 80 per cent of their non-cash payments.

17 *Ibid.*

18 These included Indian Refining Co., Copperweld Steel Co., La Clede-Christy Clay Products Co., American Asphalt Roof Corp., United Drill and Tooling Corp., and Garlock Packing Corp., Rolbein, *op. cit.*, pp. 244-45.

No adequate data are available but it is likely that the preponderance of these dividends represented distributions of investments held in other corporations, usually a subsidiary. Many cases have been uncovered of the distribution to common stockholders of common stock investments in subsidiary corporations.[19] Characteristic of these was the distribution by the Niles-Bemont-Pond Co., machine tool manufacturers, of the common stock owned in the General Machinery Corp. and in the Shepherd-Niles Crane and Hoist Company, for the express purpose of preserving the working capital of the corporation.[20] Another example is found in the case of U. S. Sugar Corporation which distributed 1/4 share of Clewiston Realty & Development Co. common on each share of common held. This amounted to $631,720 which, together with a cash dividend of $450,000, enabled U. S. Sugar Corp. to avoid the surtax entirely.[21]

Another more unusual example of tax avoidance is provided by the Mission Oil Co., of Kansas City, Missouri. This company had received $832,935 in the 4 per cent dividend notes, due 1942, of the Southwestern Development Co., a subsidiary company. After redemption of part of these notes, $688,253 in notes remained which were deposited by Mission Oil Co. with a trustee, and certificates of beneficial interest distributed as a $2 dividend on its capital stock.[22]

"Other assets" also included treasury stock of the corporation of which only six million dollars worth was distributed in 1936. While the Revenue Act of 1936 specifically authorized such distribution as constituting a *bona fide* taxable payment, its validity was subject to some uncertainty and many cautioned

19 See Rolbein, *op. cit.*, p. 241.

20 *Ibid.*, p. 241.

21 *Moody's Manual of Investments, 1937.*

22 Rolbein, *op. cit.*, p. 241.

against its distribution.[23] One factor which may have discouraged the use of treasury stock for this purpose was the 1936 change in the law with respect to the taxability of any gains arising from its sale. Since many corporations acquired much of their own stock at bargain prices during the depression period, they may have been reluctant to distribute it at the current market value, the effect of which might create a taxable profit in itself.

Unlike other forms of non-cash dividends, the potential effects on the corporation of distributions in kind were unobjectionable. As an alternative to cash dividends, the corporation realized a dividend credit without impairing its working capital. While the earning assets of the business may have been reduced, they were in effect transferred from the corporate pocket to that of the corporation owners themselves. Whereas this source of earnings may have previously been channelled through the intermediary corporation they were now received directly. So far as control over the subsidiary was concerned, it remained in the same hands as before—i.e., the owners of the holding corporation. [24]

Payments in kind were definitely limited by the nature and amount of the investments of the corporation. Only corporations with such assets could avail themselves of this opportunity for tax avoidance. Moreover, unless associated with an optional cash dividend, such investments had to possess a market for purposes of valuation. For this reason, stock of wholly owned subsidiaries was generally unavailable for distributions in kind.

23 The fact of its acquisition by the corporation obviously would not alter the proportionate interests of the stockholders in its distribution as a dividend. *Columbia Law Review*, XXXVI (1936), p. 1328.

24 An additional inducement was given to such distributions by the tax on intercorporate dividends imposed by the Revenue Act of 1935 (see *infra*, pp. 145-146). This tax advantage, amounting to a saving of 2.25 percent on dividends received, probably accounted in large part for the sizable distributions in kind made in 1936.

CHAPTER VI

THE ROLE OF THE CAPITAL MARKETS

1. The Allocation of Investment Capital

Considerations of tax equity were not the only reasons urged for the taxation of undistributed profits. While less prominent at the time of the original proposal, such reform of the tax system was also defended as a means of achieving a more efficient allocation of capital. This objective was subsequently stated by President Roosevelt in his message to Congress on April 28, 1938 which led to the Investigation of Concentration of Economic Power by the Temporary National Economic Committee.[1] The President declared, in part, that, "When it (the undistributed profits tax) was enacted two years ago, its objective was known to be closely related to the problem of concentrated economic power and a free capital market."

With the major exceptions of public utilities and railroads, American industry has expanded largely through the reinvestment of corporation earnings.[2] Institution of the tax on retained profits introduced a new and disturbing factor in the disposal of corporation earnings which raised a fundamental issue over the proper direction and control of business invest-

1 *Message from the President of the United States Transmitting Recommendations Relative to the Strengthening and Enforcement of Anti-Trust Laws*, S. Doc. No. 173, 75th Cong., 3d Sess., April 28, 1938.

2 See *Final Report of the Executive Secretary*, Temporary National Economic Committee on the Concentration of Economic Power in the United States, pp. 226-231. For example, Owen D. Young testified that of the $322,000,000 of resources owned by the General Electric Company, $192,000,000 came from undistributed profits and $92,000,000 from sale of stocks. It was reported by Alfred P. Sloan, Jr., Chairman of the Board of General Motors Corporation, that, "In the last 18 years there has been substantially no outside financing." Total funds available from internal sources aggregated $1,100,000,000 with $520,000,000 from depreciation allowances and $490,000,000 from undistributed profits. p. 227.

ment and expansion. While corporation managers attacked its alleged interference with prudent business judgment and the discouragement of investment, proponents of the surtax defended it as an instrument for democratizing corporation financial policies.

Stockholders commonly have little or no control over the disposition of their share of corporation profits. Such important policy decisions are the prerogative of the directors who are presumed to act in the best interests of the owners from whom they derive their power. Reinvestment of corporation profits may be justified in theory where the marginal rate of profit on new investment is at least equal to the return on new investment in other industries with similar risk. In practice, however, dividend policies are frequently arbitrary and often influenced by the selfish interests of management.[3] With the growth in size and concentration of industry the autocratic control over business investment by corporation management (and investment institutions) has increasingly replaced the independent forces of the market in the allocation of investment funds. The result, it is charged, is a tendency toward misdirected investment, with overexpansion of some lines and underdevelopment of others.

The taxation of undistributed profits was, therefore, defended as a positive check on the autocratic decisions to invest which characterized corporation management. To the extent corporation profits were made available to stockholders for their dis-

3 One group of businessmen has stated that, "The investment in a particular firm comes to depend in considerable part on the whim of controlling stockholders, not necessarily the majority. It depends also upon their desire for power and prestige as go with management of a large concern; and the effect which dividend payments might have in increasing their personal surtaxes." H. S. Dennison, L. Filene, R. E. Flanders, M. E. Leeds, *Toward Full Employment* (New York: McGraw-Hill Book Co., 1938), p. 232. The same point of view is also maintained by Graham and Dodd who argue that management should retain or reinvest earnings only with the specific approval of stockholders. Benjamin Graham and David L. Dodd, *Security Analysis* (New York: McGraw-Hill Book Co., 1940), pp. 382-383.

posal in the investment market, it was argued, the supply of savings would be kept in proper balance with demand, and industrial maladjustment would be minimized by the optimum allocation of funds in accordance with prospective profits. One of the principal exponents of this point of view was Rexford G. Tugwell, an economic adviser to President Roosevelt. With respect to the proper allocation of capital funds, Tugwell suggested that, " In general, the principle invoked would be to drive corporate surplus into the open investment market; for most of the trouble comes from self allocation occurring strictly within a single organization." [4] The use of the undistributed profits tax is suggested to force out these funds which " . . . would have to seek reinvestment through the regular channels, and a concern's plans for expansion would be subject to check in the investment market." [5]

However attractive this argument in theory, it should not be overlooked that the alleged discipline of the market has failed to prevent overexpansion of certain lines of industry which depend on sale of securities for their funds. Excellent examples are to be found in the case of real estate, public utilities and railroads which have traditionally relied heavily on external financing for their growth. The investment bankers whose function it is to direct the flow of capital into industry have probably been a greater source of misdirected investment and loss to investors than the optimistic directors whose decisions are, at least supported by the preponderant evidence of earnings themselves.

This opposing point of view is perhaps best expressed by the oft-quoted report of the Colwyn Committee [6] that, " When a company saves by retaining part of its profit, the operation

4 Rexford G. Tugwell, *The Industrial Discipline and the Government Arts* (New York: Columbia University Press, 1933), p. 206.

5 *Idem.*

6 *Report of the Committee on National Debt and Taxation,* Cmd. 2800, H. M. Stationery Office, London, 1927, p. 149.

is smooth and simple. In the case of a progressive business the flow of capital is just in the place where it is required; it is at the growing point of industry, enabling new needs and opportunities to be met without delay as and when they arise. This is true of the new enterprising business, which may as yet be making only small profits, as well as of the established company whose ability to save large sums for development year by year has given proof of efficiency and power of continued expansion. . . . generally speaking, it is true that the Income Tax, when it falls on company reserves, entrenches upon a form of saving which is of special value to the community."

It is the purpose of the following discussion to determine the extent to which the capital market replaced the reinvestment of corporation earnings in this period, and to examine the practicability of external financing as a means of avoiding the surtax on undistributed earnings. No attempt will be made to evaluate the influence of the surtax on the " optimum allocation " of available capital; unfortunately, no criteria have been developed which enable any positive conclusions to be made in this respect.[7]

2. The Capital Market 1936-1937

The period 1936-1937 presented the most favorable opportunity for external financing since the bull market of the 1920's. These years coincided with the highest level of national income reached within the decade of the 1930's. In 1936 the national income is estimated at $66.9 billion and in 1937 at $73.6 billion, compared with a low point of $41.7 billion in 1932 and a high of $72.5 billion in 1939.[8]

7 Some critics were concerned over the diversion of savings from investment in business to invesment in tax-exempt bonds which appeared to be taking place at this time. See, for example, Gerhard Colm and Fritz Lehmann, *Economic Consequences of Recent American Tax Policy*. Social Research, Supplement I, 1938. The limited availability of such issues, however, should have given cause for little concern in this respect.

8 *National Income*, supplement to *Survey of Current Business*, July 1947, p. 19.

TABLE NO. 14

ISSUES OF CORPORATION SECURITIES FOR NEW CAPITAL PURPOSES, 1929-1940
(Millions of dollars)

Year	Total long term issues	Long term bonds & notes	Preferred stock	Common stock	Total stock	Per cent of stock to total
1929	$7798	$1874	$1517	$4407	$5924	76.0
1930	3693	2460	412	1091	1503	40.7
1931	1262	951	116	195	311	24.6
1932	292	271	11	10	21	7.2
1933	144	24	15	105	120	83.3
1934	146	112	3	31	34	23.3
1935	393	323	55	15	70	17.8
1936	1170	817	90	263	353	30.2
1937	1178	769	205	204	409	34.7
1938	870	803	48	19	67	7.7
1939	379	282	26	71	97	25.6
1940	724	589	61	74	135	18.6

Source: Commercial and Financial Chronicle Series, *Statistical Abstract of the United States*, annual volumes.

Reflecting this recovery in business activity, the capital market also achieved its rebirth as a source of business funds. As seen by Table No. 14, corporation security flotations for new capital purposes reached approximately $1.2 billion in 1936 and 1937, and greatly exceeded any amount of new capital derived through this channel for any year since 1932. The amount offered for sale, however, fell far short of the $8.0 billion value of new securities issued in the peak year of 1929.

To what extent can this volume of new financing be accounted for by the undistributed profits tax? The answer to this question would provide a partial answer to the efficacy of the capital markets in supplanting the traditional reinvestment of corporate earnings. It is a curious coincidence that the estimated value of new capital issues of $1.2 billion was roughly equivalent to the estimated increase in cash dividends of $1.1 billion for each of these years. Analysis of the data, however, clearly indicates that only a relatively small proportion can be attributed directly or indirectly to increased dividend payments.

By far the greatest proportion of new issues (68 per cent) was in the form of corporation bonds and notes. An examination of the use of these funds clearly evidences their limited relationship to dividend disbursements. For example, Owens-Illinois Glass Company raised $15,000,000 in new capital in 1937 by the sale of 3½ per cent debentures, for the purpose of expansion. Additions to new property actually increased in value by this amount. While dividends were increased in these years with an increase in earnings, they were substantially less than the new funds derived from the sale of bonds. In the same year Phelps-Dodge Corporation issued debentures in the amount of $20,285,000 to finance the equipment and development of ore bodies in Arizona. Dividends amounted to $8,114,000, less than half the amount of the new issue.

On the other hand, it is evident that dividends would not have been possible in many cases without the successful sale of bond issues, despite the announced purpose of the new financing for capital expansion. One such case is that of the Aluminum Company of America which increased preferred dividends from $4,000,000 in 1935 to $17,500,000 in 1936—more than fourfold. For this purpose the corporation dipped into its working capital by about $10,000,000 and paid the balance out of current earnings of $22,000,000. In 1937 preferred dividends were maintained at $17,200,000 out of earnings of $27,800,000. At this time, however, the company sold $24,000,000 of 15 year debentures for the announced purpose of expansion and funding short term notes of $4,000,000. While such expansion was actually undertaken, the payment of preferred arrears would not have been possible without the funds derived from the sale of bonds. In general, however, it appears that not more than a small part of the funds derived from the sale of corporation bonds was diverted to the payment of dividends.

Analysis by industrial classification tends to confirm the

above conclusion. In 1937 the industrial breakdown of new capital issues was as follows:[9]

	Amount (millions)	Per cent
Industrial	$ 680.7	55.6
Investment Trust	0.3	0.0
Land, buildings	10.0	0.8
Public Utilities	153.3	12.5
Railroads	231.6	18.8
Miscellaneous	148.9	12.2
	$1,225.0	100.0

The issues of public utilities and railroads, accounting for $385,000,000, far exceeded the net increase in dividends estimated for these industrial groups in 1937 of less than $85,000,000. On the other hand, approximately $680,700,000, or 55.6 per cent of the total, was accounted for by industrials—substantially less than the roughly $900,000,000 increase in dividends estimated for this group. Moreover, a major portion of these securities was sold for expansion of fixed assets, with no apparent relationship to dividend payments. Among the most important of these was the $50,000,000 issue of preferred stock by E. I. du Pont de Nemours in 1937 to finance capital improvements. Dividends were increased commensurately with earnings in 1936 and 1937 to $74,000,000 and $76,700,000, respectively, from $40,800,00 in 1934 and $49,500,000 in 1935. Net working capital remained practically unchanged at the end of 1936, but by the end of 1937 it had increased by $32,600,000, largely in marketable securities, as a result of the funds derived from the sale of preferred stock. While part of these funds may have been used for dividend payments, it is clear that the major portion was held for future expenditure. Another relevant case is that of American Rolling Mills Co. which issued $44,100,000 of new preferred stock in 1937. Redemption of outstanding bonds left about $13,500,000 for new construction and working capital; after payment of dividends in 1937 of about $5,000,000

9 *Commercial and Financial Chronicle*, V. 146, Part I, p. 169.

from net income of approximately $8,300,000, working capital was actually higher by $21,600,000, including an amount of $9,000,000 described as resulting from proceeds of the sale of stock.

It is possible to estimate only very roughly the actual amount of new financing in 1936 and 1937 attributable to the undistributed profits tax. By comparison with new financing in 1939, a year comparable to 1937 in respect to the size of national income and corporate earnings, the amount would appear to be large. In other respects, however, 1939 was a year of mixed trends which contributed to an unusually low volume of new financing. War clouds were gathering on the horizon, the price level continued to decline, and, perhaps most important, the stock market failed to revive to more than 75 per cent of the 1937 peak. It was not until the last third of the year that business activity showed any marked improvement at all. Taking into account the propitious market conditions of 1936-1937 as compared to 1939, together with an analysis of the purpose of new corporate issues, it is estimated that not more than $400,000,000, or roughly one third of the new capital issues a year, can be ascribed directly or indirectly to the increased payment of dividends.[10]

3. The Sale of Common Stock by Preemptive Rights

When earnings are needed to finance working capital requirements, the conventional method of meeting dividend payments is by the sale of new stock to shareholders through the issuance of preemptive rights. In principle, the cash dividend provides the means of purchasing the stock which is issued in approximately equivalent amounts and timed to coincide with the payment of dividends.

10 Since the data reported by the *Commercial and Financial Chronicle* include only issues for public distribution, in addition to what private financing comes to its attention, they do not represent complete coverage of all issues placed privately. The volume of such private financing, though probably not very large, should also be taken into account.

The implicit value of stock rights to the stockholder in protecting his interest in the corporation from dilution provides the principal incentive to the purchase of the stock offered. Where a market exists for the stock, the new issue is ordinarily priced below the market value, thus providing a measure of explicit value to the " right." Where no market exists, " rights " may be issued at less than book value of the stock, so that its purchase may be essential to preserving one's equity in the corporation against dilution. The use of " rights " should, therefore, provide a comparatively cheap and convenient method of recouping dividends paid out as a result of the surtax on undistributed earnings. The availability of such funds for reinvestment by the shareholder, is subject, of course, to the income tax liability on the dividends received.

The tax " burden " is not only thereby distributed in accordonce with individual ability to pay, but the investor is given an opportunity to exercise his judgment with respect to reinvestment of corporate earnings. Failure to exercise the "rights" may not necessarily result in any sacrifice of his investment in the corporation if he is able to sell them for whatever value they command. In this respect investment in the corporation is put to test of the market.

Perhaps the best known example of the use of stock rights occasioned by the undistributed profits tax is the experience of Sears, Roebuck and Co. While profits of $31,511,152 had been realized in the fiscal period of 1937, the company needed these funds to finance increased inventories which were expanding in proportion to sales. In order to avoid the enormous burden of the surtax on undistributed earnings, before the end of the fiscal year, Sears, Roebuck announced the sale of new stock to its stockholders in the amount of $35,183,160.[11] These funds were used primarily to reimburse the company for divi-

11 All together $42,385,000 was brought in at this time by sale of new stock, the balance being raised from other sources, including officers and employees.

dend payments of $30,484,713 in this fiscal year, consisting of extra dividends of $1.75 per share in December and $2.50 in January, 1937, in addition to the regular quarterly dividend of 50 cents per share. The balance of the new cash raised was apparently used for working capital and dividend payments in the following year.[12]

In the same period, Montgomery Ward and Co. paid dividends of $19,318,174 which were made possible by a new common stock issue. In December, 1936, common stockholders were issued " rights " to purchase one share of stock for each seven shares held, to expire January 29, 1937. The total amount received from this issue was $24,829,320, substantially more than the dividends paid. In 1937, R. H. Macy and Co. issued " rights " for the sale of common stock in the amount of $5,564,200, out of which dividends of $3,158,653 were paid in this period. Hercules Powder Co. raised $4,471,350 by the sale of new common stock to its stockholders to enable the payments of $4,171,320 dividends in 1937. Marchant Calculating Machine Co. distributed dividends of $551,656 in 1936, which were made possible by a new stock issue of $582,804 sold to its stockholders by the use of subscription privileges.[13]

An unusual example of the issuance of " rights " to common stockholders in order to pay preferred dividends is provided by the Yellow Truck and Coach Manufacturing Co. Common and Class B stockholders were offered rights to subscribe to a $9,000,000 issue of new Class B stock. All the common stock was owned by General Motors Corporation which agreed to take all unsubscribed stock. From the proceeds of the sale, preferred arrears of $35 per share were paid in the amount

12 The above data were taken from *Moody's Manual of Investments.*

13 The above data were taken from Moody's Manual. Other examples of the use of rights in the sale of stock clearly associated with the payment of dividends are: New Britain Machine Co., Hollander & Sons, Inc., Kreuger Brewing Co., Casco Products Corp., Taylor Colquitt Co., Berghoff Brewing Corp., Emerson Electric Manufacturing Co., Cluett, Peabody & Co., Inc. See David L. Rolbein, *op. cit.*, p. 252.

of $5,039,300, compared with net income after taxes of $5,089,-024. Since General Motors owned about 70 per cent of the preferred stock, it was partially reimbursed for whatever amounts it subscribed to the new shares.

It is not possible to estimate the full effect of the undistributed profits tax on the sale of new stock issues by the use of preemptive rights. However, the evidence clearly indicates the limited exploitation of this device, despite an appreciable increase in the issuance of stock rights by listed corporations in the years 1936-1937 as shown by the following data:[14]

Year	Number of "Rights" Issues
1930	159
1931	45
1932	33
1933	26
1934	14
1935	20
1936	110
1937	110
1938	27

This tabulation is by no means complete since it is limited to stocks listed on an organized exchange or traded over the counter. It, nevertheless, provides an index of the relative importance of stock rights in 1936-1937 compared with the previous and following years. It would be incorrect, however, to attribute the increase over previous years entirely to the undistributed profits tax. In great part their increased popularity reflected the opportunity provided by the reviving stock market to finance the fixed and working capital requirements of an expanding industry. Between the period from January 1, 1936 to June 30, 1937, the total face amount of 95 such stock issues registered with the Securities and Exchange Com-

14 *Stock Rights Tables*, Commerce Clearing House, 1945.

mission is estimated at about $330,000,000.[15] The amount registered for the remainder of the year 1937 is not disclosed.

One careful survey[16] clearly associates only 41 "rights" with the undistributed profits tax over this two year period. Only 13 were definitely linked to payment of dividends by published statements of the corporations. While the standards applied in this survey were unusually rigid, an independent check confirms the limited importance of the use of preemptive rights for the purpose of tax avoidance. A most liberal estimate places the total amount of capital raised over the biennium 1936-1937 in this connection at $250,000,000—less than 50 per cent of the total value of new common stock issues in 1936-1937, and about one third of the total new capital raised by both preferred and common stock.

4. Limitations on the Use of Preemptive Rights

REGISTRATION AND OTHER EXPENSES

The issuance of new stock for public distribution ordinarily involves an impressive amount of preparation and expense which was not always justified in terms of the potential net savings in income tax. Considerably in advance of the new offering approval must be authorized by the stockholders, amendment to the charter filed, and new securities printed. Several weeks may be required to prepare audited financial statements in order to meet the requirements of the S. E. C. Registration statements must be prepared by lawyers and accountants, printed, and filed with the S. E. C.; after a waiting period of twenty days a prospectus is mailed to stockholders who are usually given from three to four weeks to exercise their rights to the new issue.

15 *Data on Certain Common Stock Issues Registered under the Securities Act of 1933 and Offered to Stockholders by Means of Rights.* Statistical Series Release No. 41, Item 1, Securities and Exchange Commission, Washington, D. C., November 29, 1937.

16 David L. Rolbein, *op. cit.*, p. 253.

The expense of this preliminary preparation is largely independent of the size of the issue. During the period in study the expense of an issue of common stock incurred in registration fees, revenue stamps, state qualifying fees, transfer agent, printing and engraving, lawyers' fees, accountants' fees, and other miscellaneous costs, averaged 1.28 per cent of the offering price.[17]

COMPENSATION TO UNDERWRITERS

The major cost, however, was involved in the distribution and sale of the securities to the stockholders and to the public. When the company wished to be relieved of the risk of its disposal, sale of the issue was usually underwritten by investment bankers. More than half of the number of issues, involving about one-half the sales value, were guaranteed by investment banking houses during this period.[18] Commissions were charged on the entire amount of the offering to cover cost of distribution, in addition to a commission on the amount not sold to shareholders which was taken up by the underwriters.

Data collected by the S. E. C. on the actual cost of underwriting new stock issues during this period show considerable variation in the commission charged [19] which ranged from 1.0 to 10.9 per cent of the value of the offering.[20] Approximately one fifth the number of issues underwritten cost from 9.0 to 11.0 per cent for commissions alone, and about two fifths cost in excess of 5.0 per cent of subscription value. These costs tended to vary inversely with the size of the issue. This is revealed by the following data on selected issues:[21]

17 M. Slade Kendrick, *The Undistributed Profits Tax*, p. 75. These data, broken down into the principal elements of cost, were supplied by the S.E.C.

18 S.E.C. *Statistical Series Release* No. 41, *loc. cit.*

19 The cost of distributing issues not underwritten is not disclosed.

20 *Ibid.*

21 *Ibid.*

Name of company	Value of offering	Compensation (per cent of value of offering)
Sears, Roebuck & Co.	$31,864,320	1.6
Continental Can Co., Inc.	10,660,740	2.3
Johns-Manville Corp.	10,000,000	1.5
American Steel Foundries	7,763,320	1.3
Inland Steel Company	6,745,500	1.4
Carnegie Metals Co.	224,246	10.0
Pfeiffer Brewing Co.	370,891	10.0
Grand National Films Inc.	409,566	10.0
Brown-Forman Distillery Co. ...	460,000	10.9
Tom Moore Distillery Co.	498.906	10.8

On the other hand, many large companies paid unusually large underwriting commissions. It cost Hupp Motor Car Co., for example, about 9.3 per cent on an issue of $3,000,000 and Union Bag and Paper Co. 5.0 per cent on an issue of $2,600,000. Other issues were underwritten either by an affiliated company, or officers and directors, without commission. To all these commission charges should be added the expense of preparation and registration, which averaged about 1.3 per cent. The complete cost to Sears, Roebuck, for example, was reported to be $803,047, which amounted to 1.9 per cent of its entire new issue, compared with the underwriting commission alone on part of the issue of 1.6 per cent.[22] Monsanto Chemical Company reported an underwriting cost of 2.5 per cent, but the entire cost was 3.1 per cent.[23]

However large these financing costs are, they range appreciably below the average cost of floating new issues of stock which are not sold to security holders with the use of " rights ".[24] This is confirmed by a comparison of the cost of

22 *Annual Report* of Sears, Roebuck & Co., 1937.

23 *Moody's Manual of Investments*, 1938.

24 *Cf.* the estimates submitted by M. Slade Kendrick, *op. cit.*, p. 77. The average quarterly spread in underwriting new issues of common stock during this period is reported by Dr. Kendrick to be between 13.1 and 15.2 per cent. Presumably the estimates are based on the cost of selling *all* new issues of stock, including unseasoned securities and new ventures, both to stockholders and to the public—not strictly comparable with financing additional capital requirements of established companies.

flotation of various types of distribution during the period 1938-1939. In 1938 the average cost of flotation for securities underwritten to security holders (i.e., by the use of "rights") was 2.9 per cent of preferred stock sold, and 8.1 per cent of common stock sold. In 1939, the respective percentages were 2.6 per cent and 3.5 per cent. The sale of many issues was apparently underwritten at little or no cost to the corporation. As seen by the accompanying Table 15, the average cost of distributing all issues offered to stockholders was substantially less than the cost of selling issues directly to the public, both underwritten and non-underwritten.

TABLE NO. 15

COST OF FLOTATION AS PER CENT OF AMOUNT SOLD

	1938		1939	
	Common	Preferred	Common	Preferred
Underwritten:				
To security holders .	8.1%	2.9%	3.5%	2.6%
To public	22.6	4.3	16.9	6.3
Non-underwritten	20.8	14.0	19.0	16.0

Source: *Cost of Flotation for Registered Securities 1938-1939.* S.E.C. (Washington, D. C.), March, 1941, pp. 8-9.

While the average cost of underwriting was not large, it, nevertheless, represented an expensive method of "compliance" with the undistributed profits tax in many cases. In the case of small unseasoned issues particularly, the expense of selling new stock to shareholders by the use of rights was an important deterrent to the employment of this device for tax avoidance. While the maximum surtax rate was 27 per cent, the net saving in taxes represented by "underwriting" the payment of dividends often did not justify this technique, particularly in view of the alternative tax to the individual dividend recipient.

SECURITIES NOT UNDERWRITTEN

On the other hand, many corporations were able to sell substantial amounts of common stock directly to their shareholders without incurring the costs of underwriting. Such sales were facilitated by a discount from market price generally in excess of that employed in cases of underwriting. The size of some of these issues was also appreciably greater than those underwritten during the same period. Among the more important sales of common stocks not underwritten in 1936 and 1937 were the following:[25]

Name of company	Value of offering	Initial discount
The Texas Corporation	$62,267,760	26.1%
Montgomery Ward	26,085,720	39.4
American Smelting and Refining	25,619,160	23.7
Phillips Petroleum	8,898,930	30.0
Philip Morris	5,193,300	48.7

Substantially all of these issues were taken up by stockholders. The percentage not sold by the above listed companies ranged from nil in the case of Philip Morris to 2.5 per cent in the case of Phillips Petroleum.[26]

Securities not underwritten may or may not be sold through investment banking facilities. When employed, the investment banker simply acts as a sales agent on a commission basis. Unfortunately, data are unavailable for 1936 or 1937 on the relative importance of such sales by investment houses; in 1938, however, only a small portion of the sales of common stocks to security holders which were not underwritten was sold through investment banking facilities. The average compensation for these sales was 1.7 per cent, a relatively minor amount considering the small size of the issues. The experience

25 S.E.C. *Statistical Series Release No. 41, loc. cit.*

26 It is interesting to note that approximately $56 million out of $128 million raised by these five companies was employed to pay off bank loans, funded debt and to redeem preferred stock. The balance was employed for new investment and working capital purposes and presumably made earnings available for dividends. In the case of The Texas Corporation, for example, the balance left after repayment of bank loans and funded debt was $25.7 million, almost equivalent to the dividends paid in 1937 of $26.4 million. (*Moody's Manual of Investments,* 1938.)

in 1939 was comparable.[27] No data are available on the selling expense to the corporation for issues sold directly without the employment of selling agents, but the costs were presumably less than 1.7 per cent, particularly for large issues.

CONDITION OF THE SECURITY MARKETS

A critical factor in the successful use of rights is the pricing of the new subscription sufficiently below the market value to make it attractive to stockholders and other prospective buyers. Not only must this price be set in advance of the effective date but it must anticipate any fluctuations in market price between then and the expiration date, usually one month. In periods of rising security prices and favorable market conditions, common stock may, of course, be sold more readily than during a declining market. Even in a good market, however, unfortunate pricing of the new subscription may result in an unsuccessful sale to stockholders. During the period from January, 1936 to June, 1937, which was the crest of the speculative wave, only a fraction of many offerings was taken up because of a narrowing of the discount between the subscription and market price. A few of these are summarized as follows: [28]

Name of company	Effective date	Per cent taken by stock-holders	Discount	
			Regis-tration date	Expira-tion date
General Time Instruments Co.	4/15/36	27.7%	6.0%	0.0%
Globe Steel Tubes Co.	6/28/37	38.7	7.1	a
Hupp Motor Car Corp.	4/19/37	21.2	a	4.0
Mar-Tex Oil Co.	2/25/37	3.4	0.0	4.0
Pfeiffer Brewing Co.	4/ 8/37	61.2	10.6	a
Union Bag and Paper Co.	4/17/36	45.0	13.0	0.0
Berghoff Brewing Corp.	4/23/37	50.6	11.1	0.0
California Engels Mining Co.	6/17/37	30.2	0.0	0.0

a Market price below subscription price.

27 *Cost of Flotation for Registered Securities 1938-1939*, Securities and Exchange Commission, Washington, D. C., March 1941, p. A-1.

28 S.E.C. *Statistical Series Release No. 41, loc. cit.*

With the stock market decline which took place during the last quarter of 1937 the situation was even more serious. While particular data are lacking, studies of the S. E. C. show that only 20 per cent of unseasoned securities registered during this period were sold, compared with 60 per cent sold during the first quarter of 1937.[29] It is also known that many proposed new issues were actually withdrawn with the break in the market during the latter part of 1937. A notable instance was the withdrawal of a new offering of common stock by the Phillips Petroleum Company on September 27, 1937, because of "unfavorable market conditions." [30] This company had successfully sold a large issue of common stock to its shareholders in September, 1936, ostensibly to pay dividends; while it was not underwritten, the unsubscribed shares were purchased at the market by an investment banking house. When an attempt was made to repeat this performance exactly one year later, with the assistance of underwriters, the decline in the market price of its stock which accompanied the business recession forced a cancellation of these plans. Shortly thereafter the corporation placed privately with two insurance companies $9,000,000 in notes, maturing serially through December 1, 1945.[31]

The successful distribution of new stock issues is, therefore, contingent upon favorable market conditions. Since dividend credit was given only for dividends distributed in the taxable year, a sudden drop in the stock market during the year militated against further possible use of stock purchase rights. Had the undistributed profits tax been retained in 1938, the employment of stock "rights" might have been seriously handicapped by the depressed securities markets during most of this year.

29 *Sales Record of Unseasoned Registered Securities 1933-1939.* S.E.C. (Washington, D. C.), June, 1941.

30 *Commercial and Financial Chronicle,* Vol. 145, p. 2239.

31 *Ibid.*, p. 3828.

5. The Experience with Convertible Bonds and Preferred Stock

In 1936 and 1937 an unusual number of convertible preferred stock and bond issues were offered to stockholders by the use of preemptive rights. Provision was made for their conversion into common stock at favorable rates at the option of the holder. A speculative element was thus added to the current factor of safety in enabling investors to benefit from any future appreciation in the common stock of the corporation.

Analysis of the major convertible issues floated in 1937 shows that their principal purpose was refunding and refinancing. In most cases, however, substantial new funds were received for working capital purposes. While the new capital made it possible to distribute a substantial portion of the earnings, which might otherwise have been retained for working capital, about one-half of the companies studied paid a surtax on undistributed profits. (The taxable profits of some companies included apparently were considerably less than the profits reported to stockholders.) Allis-Chalmers, for example, obtained about $13,000,000 in new funds from a $25,330,000 convertible debenture issue in 1937, but only $6,200,000 was distributed out of $8,500,000 earnings reported, the balance being subject to a surtax of $665,000.[32] At the same time, net working capital was increased by $22,700,000 in 1937. Thus, many corporations in need of increased working capital were enabled to distribute sufficient earnings to avoid the higher surtax rates by floating convertible issues which were large enough to obtain additional working capital and to refinance outstanding issues as well. Presumably the surtax rate on earnings retained was balanced against the additional cost of financing a larger issue, both with respect to cost of flotation and possibly higher charges for interest or preferred dividends.

32 *Moody's Manual of Investments*, 1938.

Offerings of convertible securities are no less subject to the hazards of the market than sales of common stock. In 1937 many such issues remained undigested for long periods of time and serious losses were experienced by the underwriters. This experience is exemplified by the distribution of 442,443 shares of Pure Oil Company 5 per cent convertible preferred stock offered to common stockholders September 3, 1939. As a result of a sharp break in the market, only 8,049 shares were subscribed to and the underwriters had to take up the balance at $97.50 a share. More than a year after the original offering it was estimated that the members of the syndicate still held 168,200 shares which sold on that date at 80¾.[33] As a result of this and many other similar instances, it has been claimed that the largest losses incurred by underwriters have been in connection with convertible issues offered first to old security holders.[34] Despite the evidence presented of many instances of presumed losses, it is difficult to reconcile this bad record with the relatively low average underwriting commission charged.[35]

33 T. Kenneth Haven, *Investment Banking under the Securities and Exchange Commission*, Michigan Business Studies, Vol. IX, No. 3 (University of Michigan, Ann Arbor, 1940), p. 73.

34 *Ibid.*, p. 76.

35 Typical underwriting commissions ranged from 1.1 per cent for convertible bonds, with 3.1 per cent charged for any unsubscribed portion, to 1.9 per cent for preferred stock, with 2.9 per cent charged for the amount taken up by the syndicate. *Cost of Flotation for Registered Securities 1938-1939*. S.E.C., March, 1941, p. 3.

CHAPTER VII

THE EFFECT ON BUSINESS GROWTH AND MONOPOLY

1. The Plight of Small Business

Taxes on corporation income may limit the growth of business in two ways: They may impair incentives to expand and they may curtail corporation funds available for investment. The graduated surtax on undistributed profits not only introduced a new restraint on incentives to invest but also contributed to a reduction in corporation funds available for investment by an amount greater than the tax itself. In both these respects the undistributed profits tax tended to discourage the development of small and medium size businesses, which are most dependent upon the reinvestment of earnings for growth. The *incentive* given to distribution of earnings for the purpose of tax avoidance, however, was the principal deterrent to new investment; the amount of tax on earnings retained represented a relatively small percentage of corporation income.

If the impact of the tax is measured by the amount of readjustment entailed in the financial policies and practices of business, the small and medium size corporations were hardest hit. This is clearly evidenced by a comparison of the dividend record of small and large corporations before and after the tax, as presented in Chapter II. Here it was explained how the increase in dividend payments by small and medium size busiesses was proportionately greater than in the case of large business. While the increased disbursements were compelled by the desire to minimize taxes, the premium placed on distribution, nevertheless, discouraged the direct flow of reinvested earnings which has provided the major source of business expansion.

The dependence of American business on internal growth is well known. For most companies it is the only source of expansion, whose importance varies with the size of the corporation. Interesting new evidence of the relatively greater dependence of small business on the reinvestmnt of profits is presented in a survey undertaken by Dun & Bradstreet in 1937. Their inquiry into the origin of increases in net worth between 1920 and 1928 of 365 companies sampled disclosed that retained earnings were the only source of increased net worth for 84 per cent of small companies, 71 per cent of medium size concerns, and 60 per cent of large corporations.[1]

Little is known of the extent to which investment by small and medium size businesses was actually inhibited by the undistributed profits tax. Several inquiries at the time indicated a rather widespread curtailment of plant expenditure, but the amount was not disclosed. A survey of 3,000 companies by the Illinois Manufacturers Association, for example, indicated that 83 per cent of the respondents had deferred or abandoned plans for plant expansion or rehabilitation because of the tax.[2] On the basis of a similar analysis one widely circulated report concluded that the undue restrictions placed on the expansion of industry made its repeal imperative.[3] Because of the hostility of business toward the surtax such replies are subject to considerable discount but obviously cannot be ignored. It is the purpose of the present Chapter to examine the possible discrimination of the surtax against the growth of new and small business and the possible encouragement given to monopoly and concentration in industry.

2. The Problem of Capital

ACCESSIBILITY OF OUTSIDE CAPITAL

The reinvestment of earnings by small and many medium size businesses is attributable partly to choice and partly to

1 W. L. Thorp and E. B. George, "An Appraisal of the Undistributed Profits Tax," *Dun's Review*, September, 1937, p. 23.

2 *Hearings before the Committee on Ways and Means, Revenue Revision Laws 1938*, p. 775.

3 M. Slade Kendrick, *op. cit.*, p. 92.

economic circumstances. Probably most close corporations are owned by families or close business associates who are loathe to distribute shares to the public because of fear of surrendering control to investment bankers and others. They have a sentimental attachment to a business which was privately fostered and resent the possible loss of independence which is associated with public ownership.

More important, however, is the elementary fact that the size of the business itself effectively limits public offering of securities. One authority testified that an average annual income of $200,000 sets a practical minimum below which public distribution of securities is not feasible.[4] This is obviously much above the limits of what is popularly considered to be "small business." Even when the possibility of public sale offers itself, investment bankers are reluctant to handle small issues because of the limited opportunities for profit and high risks of disposal. One study of the S. E. C. disclosed that only 40 per cent of the amount of securities registered by small going concerns in 1935-1939 were actually sold.[5]

The high cost of selling reflects the low rate of absorption of such issues. Analysis of registration statements filed with the S. E. C. in 1938 and 1939 shows that the cost of floating new issues of all types varied inversely with the size of the issuer. Data for issues non-under-written by investment bankers are presented in the accompanying Table No. 16. In 1939, a relatively good year, the cost of selling common stock by the smallest companies listed (less than $1,000,000 assets) averaged 24.1 per cent of the amount actually sold, compared to 10.9 per cent for the $5,000,000-10,000,000 company and only 4.8 per cent for the $10,000,000-50,000,000 company. A similar differential existed for preferred stock. Even these smallest

4 James J. Minot, Jr., Vice-President of the Investment Bankers Association of America, *Hearings before the Committee on Ways and Means, Revenue Revision Laws 1938*, p. 379.

5 *Sales Record of Unseasoned Registered Securities 1933-1939*, Securities and Exchange Commission, Washington, D. C., June, 1941, p. 2.

companies lie outside the commonly accepted limits of small business but they illustrate the handicap faced in the capital market.

TABLE NO. 16

TOTAL COST OF FLOTATION OF NEW SECURITIES, BY TYPE OF SECURITY AND SIZE OF ISSUER, 1938-1939

Asset size (In thousands)	Cost as per cent of amount					
	Common [a]		Preferred [a]		Bonds [b]	
	1938	1939	1938	1939	1938	1939
Under $1,000 ..	21.7	24.1	18.8	23.5	8.8	7.3
1,000- 5,000 ..	20.9	20.3	10.2	12.9	5.5	6.4
5,000-10,000 ..	14.8	10.9	11.2	8.5	5.2	3.1
10,000-50,000 ..	...	4.8	4.9	6.1	3.5	3.0

Source: S.E.C., *Cost of Flotation for Registered Securities, 1938-1939* (March, 1941), pp. 25-26.

[a] Non-underwritten to public.

[b] Underwritten to public.

EARNINGS RETAINED BY SMALL BUSINESS

Small corporations (with net income below $50,000) retained a much higher proportion of their net income available for dividends than any other net income group of corporations. As shown by Table No. 17, the undistributed profits of this small income group, amounting to $336.7 million in 1937, was 41.2 per cent of their net income available for dividends.[6] Corporations earning between $50,000 and $1,000,000 retained a uniform rate of about 20 per cent of their net income after normal and excess profits taxes; companies earning between $1,000,000 and $5,000,000, and in excess of $5,000,000, retained an average of only 13.6 per cent and 11.6 per cent, respectively, of their net income available for dividends.

Despite the fact that the smallest income group retained a larger portion of earnings than higher income groups, they paid the lowest average rate of surtax on their retention. The com-

6 Undistributed profits include only those profits retained by corporations paying the surtax; that is, the amount is not offset by dividends in excess of earnings for the year by those corporations paying no surtax. The amount retained includes the specific dividend credit as well as credit for contracts restricting payment of dividends.

pensatory tax was only 8.4 per cent of undistributed earnings, compared to an average of about 13 per cent paid by corporations in higher income classes (except for the highest class which paid 10.4 per cent). The preferential treatment accorded small companies is perhaps best emphasized by the fact that the

TABLE NO. 17

UNDISTRIBUTED PROFITS AND SURTAX PAID, BY INCOME CLASS
Corporations Subject to Surtax—1937

	Net income class (Thousands of dollars)				
	Under 50	50 to 250	250 to 1000	1000 to 5000	Over 5000
	(Millions of dollars)				
Net income [1]	916.1	1,141.2	1,389.1	1,988.5	3,767.3
Normal and excess profits taxes	99.6	145.4	206.3	242.0	400.1
Net income available for dividends [2]	816.5	995.8	1,182.8	1,746.6	3,367.2
Undistributed profits [3]	336.7	239.3	261.0	273.1	436.9
Surtax paid	28.4	32.3	34.3	35.4	45.6
Profits retained after surtax	308.3	207.0	226.7	237.7	391.3
	Per cent				
Per cent undistributed profits to income available for dividends	41.2	20.8	19.1	13.6	11.6
Per cent surtax to undistributed profits	8.4	13.5	13.1	12.9	10.4

Source: *Statistics of Income for 1937*, pp. 11-14; Treasury Department.

[1] Net income for "declared value" excess profits tax computation.

[2] Similar to "adjusted net income" except for interest on certain government obligations and credits allowed certain holding company affiliates and to national mortgage associations.

[3] Net income retained by companies with surtax, including estimated credit for contracts restricting payment of dividends by all companies (Table No. 11) and specific credit for corporations with net income below $50,000 (Table No. 18).

lowest income group was able to withhold from distribution an appreciably greater absolute amount of net income, at a lower tax, than the second largest income group (earning between $1,000,000 and $5,000,000) which reported more than twice as much aggregate net income.

RELIEF FOR SMALL BUSINESS

The Revenue Act of 1936 alleviated the impact of both the normal and surtax on small business. For the first time a graduated rate schedule was put into effect for small corporations, with rates graduated from 8 per cent on net income below $2,000; 11 per cent on amounts between $2,000 and $15,000; 13 per cent on net income between $15,000 and $40,000, to the maximum rate of 15 per cent on the excess over $40,000.

In addition, corporations with an adjusted net income of less than $50,000 were entitled to a specific dividend credit in computing their surtax. This credit amounted to $5,000, or the undistributed net income, whichever was less, minus 10 per cent of the undistributed net income.[7] The specific credit was subject, however, to the lowest surtax rate of 7 per cent. This represented a substantial tax saving on relatively small net incomes. For example, a corporation could withhold distribution of a net income of $10,000, after normal taxes, by payment of an effective surtax rate of only 12.5 per cent instead of the 20.5 per cent applicable to large corporations. The specific credit amounted to $4,000, or 40 per cent of its adjusted net income ($5,000 less 10 per cent of $10,000). Since the amount of $4,000 was taxed at 7 per cent instead of 27 per cent (the surtax rate on the last 40 per cent of net income) the maximum marginal rate paid was 21 per cent. The tax saving was, therefore, $800, or 8 per cent of adjusted net income.

Table No. 18 presents an analysis of the amount of specific credit claimed in 1936 and 1937 by size of income and maximum surtax rate class. The total amount of credit taken of benefit to the corporation is estimated at $47.5 million in 1936 and $49 million in 1937. The credit apparently was of no benefit to corporations with net income of less than $5,000. In 1937 it amounted to about 18 per cent of the adjusted net income of the $5,000-10,000 income class, and about 8 per cent of the adjusted net income of the $10,000-$25,000 income class. As expected, it represented considerably less benefit, about 2.3 per cent, to the largest net income group entitled to the credit.

7 *Revenue Act of 1936*, Sec. 14(c).

TABLE NO. 18

AMOUNT AND DISTRIBUTION OF THE SPECIFIC CREDIT BY INCOME CLASS AND MAXIMUM SURTAX RATES, 1936-1937
(Thousands of dollars)

Income class [1]	Maximum surtax rates					Total
	7% [2]	12%	17%	22%	27%	
			1936			
Under $5	...	....	....	....	....	.....
5- 10	478	6,124	8,556	5,098	....	20,256
10- 25	142	3,977	4,727	3,915	7,486	20,247
25- 50	12	1,540	2,063	1,302	1,858	6,775
50-100	1	49	60	38	43	191
Total	632	11,691	15,406	10,353	9,386	47,468
			1937			
Under $5	...	....	....	....	....	.....
5- 10	298	7,265	8,427	5,130	....	21,120
10- 25	75	4,330	5,073	4,238	7,514	21,230
25- 50	18	1,464	2,237	1,475	1,947	7,141
50-100	1	45	66	48	47	207
Total	392	13,105	15,802	10,890	9,507	49,696

Source: Treasury Department.

[1] Net income for excess-profits tax computation.

[2] Returns with adjusted net income of under $5,000 not included where credit is of no benefit to taxpayers.

The adequacy of the relief afforded small business by the specific credit is open to some question. Due to the interpretation by the Treasury Department of the ambiguous wording of the law, it proved to be much less than expected. The law provided that the specific credit should be equal to " . . . the portion of the undistributed net income which is in excess of 10 percentum of the adjusted net income and not in excess of $5,000."[8] While this could easily be interpreted to mean that the credit should not exceed $5,000, the Treasury Department ruled that it was equal to the undistributed profits *or* $5,000 (whichever is less) *minus* 10 per cent of the adjusted net income.[9] Consequently, the full benefit of the tax relief was limited to corporations with an adjusted net income of $10,000 or less; for example, a corporation with an adjusted net income of

8 Sec. 14(c).

9 *Regulations 94*, Art. (14c).

$20,000 was not entitled to a $5,000 specific credit (if it retained all its income) but to a credit of only $3,000 ($5,000 less 10 per cent of $20,000). The amount of tax relief was, therefore, only $600 instead of $1,000, a difference of $400.

While small corporations were enabled to retain a substantially greater amount of net income at a much lower average rate of tax than large companies, they also experienced a much greater curtailment in undistributed profits. Whether sufficient recognition was given to the handicaps they experienced in securing equity capital from external sources must be weighed against considerations of tax equity. It was essentially a question of the extent to which the corporation device should be encouraged as an instrument of business promotion by the exercise of certain privileges and exemptions not enjoyed by partnerships and proprietorships. Whether as a result of political expediency or recognition of real hardships experienced under the tax laws, the Administration acknowledged that the undistributed profits tax gave inadequate consideration to small businesses,[10] and it is known that proposals were made to liberalize the specific exemption by extending a maximum credit of $5,000 to corporations with net income up to $100,000 instead of $50,000.

3. Mitigating Factors—Stock Subscriptions

On the other hand, the small concern enjoyed an advantage over the large listed corporation in recapturing the dividends distributed. Because of the close identification of ownership with management and the restricted ownership of small cor-

10 See, for example, the *Message from the President of the United States Transmitting Recommendations Relative to the Strengthening and Enforcement of Anti-Trust Laws* (S. Doc. No. 173, 75th Cong., 3d Sess.), April 29, 1938. The President stated, "It is true that the form of the 1936 tax worked a hardship on many of the smaller corporations." In 1938, Under-Secretary of the Treasury, R. Magill, recommended to the Committee on Ways and Means that complete exemption from the revised undistributed profits tax be given to corporations with incomes below $25,000. *Hearings, Revenue Revision Laws, 1938*, p. 104.

porations, resubscription to corporate stock could be initially agreed upon as a prerequisite to dividend payments. The close community of interest, frequently among members of the same family, could facilitate this process with little or no actual loss in the use of the funds. While the process of reinvestment may have suffered some delay, in many instances the transaction could be completed at a stockholders meeting.[11]

A contributing factor was the situation itself which stimulated the distribution of earnings. The fact that the ownership of small corporations tended to be concentrated more in the lower income groups than the ownership of larger and better established companies, made it more advantageous to distribute rather than reinvest earnings. Because of the comparative tax savings, the payment of dividends on condition of their reinvestment was not only facilitated but the amount remaining after payment of personal income taxes was relatively greater, on the average, than in the case of larger corporations.[12]

With progression in size, however, the problem of achieving a coordinated dividend-tax program increased. Ranging between the small individual or family company and the large public owned corporation lies an intermediate group which combines some of the limitations and advantages of each. Ownership was neither sufficiently homogeneous to permit unity of action nor the corporation large enough to warrant public sale of shares. Participation of outsiders essential to supply initial or expansion capital requirements engendered separation between management and ownership and created the possibility of greater conflicts of interest with respect to reinvestment of earnings. Such corporations were probably con-

11 The "consent dividend" privilege, then in effect under Sec. 102 and later extended in the Revenue Revision Act of 1938, would have greatly expedited this process.

12 An individual with a net taxable income of $6,000 before dividends would be subject to an additional tax of only 9 per cent on dividends of $2,000 whereas an income of $50,000 would be subject to an additional tax of 35 per cent on the same amount.

fronted with the most serious problems in the application of the undistributed profits tax.

Subscription to stock by the use of quasi-coercive " rights " probably provided the best solution where stock dividends proved to be impracticable. Pricing of such rights appreciably below the book value (where no market existed) could offer a compelling incentive to reinvestment of dividends. Where such inducements proved ineffective, it was questionable whether management was justified in carrying out its investment program.

The importance of external sources of capital to corporations of various income size subject to the surtax is shown by Table No. 19. In 1936, corporations with net income below $10,000 acquired $43,012,000 in funds from the sale of common stock; including preferred stock the total was $56,700,000. This amounted to about 41.5 per cent of cash dividends paid out by this group. On the other hand, corporations with net income between $10,000 and $100,000 acquired $100,200,000 of new

TABLE NO. 19

CHANGES IN AMOUNT OF OBLIGATIONS AND CAPITAL STOCK
Corporations Subject to the Surtax on Undistributed Profits, 1936
(Thousands of dollars)

Net income class	Total	Obligations	Preferred stock	Common stock
Cash receipts from sale of corporations' obligations and capital stock				
Under $10	88,634	31,964	13,658	43,012
10-100	209,360	109,164	29,080	71,116
100 & over	3,757,482	2,959,518	266,655	531,309
Total	4,055,476	3,100,646	309,393	645,437
Cash expenditures for purchase of corporations' own obligations and capital stock				
Under $10	104,703	37,683	8,391	58,629
10-100	260,593	135,795	47,348	77,450
100 & over	3,184,512	2,680,857	326,382	177,273
Total	3,549,808	2,854,335	382,121	313,352
Net increase or decrease (—)				
Under $10	—16,072	— 5,720	5,267	—15,619
10-100	—51,234	—26,633	—18,268	— 6,333
100 & over	572,974	278,662	—59.725	354,037
Total	505,668	246,309	—72,726	332,085

Source: Treasury Department.

funds from the sale of capital stock, amounting to only 15.0 per cent of their cash dividends. The largest group of corporations, with net income above $100,000, disposed of $798,-000,000 in value of new capital stock during 1936, an amount equal to 14.8 per cent of their cash dividends. If these data are taken at their face value, it would appear that the ability of the very small corporations to secure equity funds greatly exceeded that of both the large and medium size corporations.

If funds received from the sale of corporation obligations with maturities of over one year are included, the picture is somewhat altered. Very small companies secured funds aggregating 65.2 per cent of their dividend payments, compared to 69.6 per cent received by the largest group. The relative situation of medium income companies, however, was not improved with cash receipts equivalent to only 31.5 per cent of their cash dividend payments. The data, therefore, seem to bear out the *a priori* conclusions advanced above that the medium size corporations are too large to enjoy the advantages of close relationship among their stockholders and too small to take advantage of the capital markets.

It is not possible to determine the extent to which the receipt of these funds was associated with the payment of dividends. Many net income corporations which sold securities probably did not declare any dividends at all; many others probably distributed more than the amount of cash received in the sale of securities. In large part, these funds were also employed for retirement of bank loans and other securities, particularly bonds and preferred stock.

In the aggregate, however, the above data evidenced an unusual ability of very small income corporations to secure capital by the sale of securities, despite their handicap in the capital markets. For income classes below and above $100,000 net income the amount of new funds acquired from sale of capital stock amounted to 19.6 per cent and 14.8 per cent, respectively, of cash dividend payments. On the other hand, such statistical averages ignore the handicaps of individual corporations and may conceal an inordinate amount of distress and difficulty in the process of recapturing dividends. The intermediate size corporation, in particular, appears to have been at a serious disadvantage.

4. The "Liquidation" of Small Corporations

The sale of new issues presents only one side of the coin. The obverse side is equally significant to an analysis of the growth of small versus large business. During the same period of 1936 corporations subject to the surtax on undistributed profits expended huge sums on the retirement of their own obligations and capital stock. The total amount reported for this purpose was $3,549.8 million, compared to total funds received from sale of new issues of $4,055.5 million. There remained a net increase in external funds of $505.6 million for all companies subject to the surtax, represented by net increases of $332.1 million in common stock and $246.3 million in obligations with maturity of over one year, against which there was a net reduction of $72.7 million in preferred stock outstanding. Outside funds derived from the sale of securities thus contributed to a net expansion in business assets of half a billion dollars in 1936 for this group of companies subject to the surtax.

Despite the considerable increase in capitalization for all companies included, corporations with net income below $100,000 suffered a net decline of $67.3 million. The implications of this situation for the development of small business, unfortunately, are not entirely clear because of the inadequacy of the data. The most likely explanation of the decline in capitalization of small businesses is summarized below.

It was assumed in the preceding discussion that receipts from the sale of new securities were employed largely for new capital purposes. This implies that the sale and redemption of securities were conducted independently by entirely different corporations. Actually, it is known that extensive refunding operations were conducted in 1936 and that corporations sold new bonds and stock for the purpose of redeeming old bonds and bank loans. This is evidenced by the fact that total new capital received from the sale of securities in this year was near $1.2 billion—considerably less than the $4.0 billion shown in Table 19.

On the other hand, there is a strong presumption that the receipts of cash from the sale of stocks and bonds devoted to new capital purposes greatly exceeded the *net* increase in funds received. It is rather improbable, for example, that stocks and bonds would be issued for the retirement of other stocks, particularly common stocks, the total redemption value of which amounted to $645.4 million. Therefore, while refunding of bonds (and retirement of preferred) may have absorbed a substantial part of the proceeds from the sale of new issues, it seems clear that much new capital was raised for other purposes.

At the same time, a substantial part of the funds employed for the purchase of corporations' own obligations and stock must have been provided from the internal resources of the corporations themselves. These funds were provided in part out of earnings or unexpended depreciation allowances. Complete or partial liquidation of corporation assets also probably supplied a large portion of the cash expenditures.

The possible effect of the undistributed profits tax on the liquidation of corporations is open to question.[13] Many critics have charged the law with fostering the development of monopolies because of the discrimination of the tax against the growth of small business. Since the evidence of Table 19 points to a net decline in capitalization of small business, attributable in part to the consolidation of small business units

13 While it might be reasoned that the increased taxation of corporation income stimulated a conversion to the partnership form, such transfer would not have been accompanied by an actual exchange of cash. Moreover, it is generally conceded that no significant trend in this direction took place. See Willard L. Thorp and Edward B. George, *op. cit.*, p. 23.

into larger ones, the claim appears to have superficial substantiation in fact. However, this inference is inconclusive—the surtax had been in effect far too short a time (in 1936) to have played any significant part in merger or consolidation. It might, indeed, have hastened those already in negotiation, or given a stimulus to others by reason of possible financial advantages. But such benefits are incidental to the real motives in consolidations which tend to be promoted during a period of business recovery and a favorable stock market which characterized 1936.

In fact, there does not appear to have been any unusual merger activity in 1936 and 1937 as evidenced by the experience of manufacturing and mining companies. The number of such companies disappearing in 1936 and 1937 averaged only 125 compared to 1,245 in 1929, 789 in 1930, and 101 in 1934 and 130 in 1935.[14] On the other hand, activity may have been accelerated in other fields for which there are no adequate records, for example, retailing, hotels and motion pictures.

To attribute the liquidation of small corporations to the impact of the surtax is a highly oversimplified explanation which ignores more relevant developments in the taxation of corporations. One factor which encouraged mergers and sale of assets was the liberalized treatment of profits resulting from liquidation of corporations which were not controlled subsidiaries. Whereas gains arising from complete liquidation of corporations were previously fully taxable, the Revenue Act of 1936 permitted such profits to be taxed under the capital gains provision which reduced the amount taxable in accordance with the length of period the stock was held.[15] Complete liquidation was defined to include any one of a series of distributions made by a corporation in redemption of *all* of its stock in accordance with a *bona fide* plan of dissolution under which the transfer

14 Willard L. Thorp and Walter F. Crowder, *The Structure of Industry*, T.N.E.C. Monograph No. 27 (Washington, D. C., 1941), p. 233.

15 Sec. 115(c).

of property was completed within a period of two years. Since the holding period percentage of capital gains taxed was graduated down to 30 per cent if held for a period of ten years or more, this provision probably encouraged the dissolution of corporations previously deterred by the high surtax rates on 100 per cent of the gain. According to one tax expert, it was expected to result in wholesale dissolution of many private investment companies.[16] It doubtless facilitated other liquidations as well.

The taxation of intercorporate dividends and the liberalized provisions for treatment of gains and losses in liquidation of controlled subsidiaries also encouraged the outright merger of affiliated companies. The Revenue Act of 1935 (which was superseded by the Act of 1936) first imposed a tax on intercorporate dividends by allowing a credit for only 90 per cent of dividend income; in 1936 the credit was reduced to 85 per cent, thus subjecting intercorporate dividends to a maximum normal tax of 2.25 per cent.[17] Dissolution of controlled subsidiaries had previously been discouraged, however, by the recognition of a taxable gain or loss, as in the case of liquidation of any company. The Revenue Act of 1935 provided for the tax-free dissolution of a controlled subsidiary which was limited to those undertaken by the exchange of property *other than money*.[18] This deterrent was finally removed by the Revenue Act of 1936 which provided that no gain or loss be recognized upon the dissolution of a controlled subsidiary, whether or not cash was involved in the transfer of assets;[19] the basis to the parent of the property received was the same as it was in the hands of the subsidiary. These provisions simplified the dissolution of

16 Joseph J. Klein, "Liquidation under the Revenue Act of 1936," *The Tax Magazine*, November, 1936, p. 648.

17 Elimination of the privilege of filing consolidated returns in 1934 also made holding company consolidations less advantageous than previously.

18 Section 112(b) (6).

19 *Revenue Act of 1936, Regulations 94*, Art. 112(b).

subsidiaries and made it possible to avoid the tax on inter-company dividends without incurring a tax on the dissolution itself.[20] Such facilitating legislation probably accounted in some part for the rather considerable amount of stock liquidations reported by all companies, and small companies in particular, in 1936.

It may reasonably be inferred from the circumstances and known facts of the situation that the liquidation of small corporations was encouraged less by the undistributed profits tax than by the liberalized provisions of the tax law with respect to the recognition of a gain (or loss) on the transaction. This was consistent with the policy of the Administration to discourage holding company consolidations by the elimination of consolidated returns and the taxation of inter-company dividends. No unusual merger activity in the industrial field was detected in 1936 or 1937, but there may have been a greater development in other fields of which there are no adequate data.

5. Effect on Business Concentration

Considerable concern was expressed over the potential effects of the undistributed profits tax in limiting the growth of small enterprise and thereby contributing to the concentration in control of business. The President specifically included in the program of the Temporary National Economic Committee an analysis of the influence of tax policy on the development of monopolies; and the undistributed profits tax was singled out for special consideration.[21]

Testimony before the T. N. E. C. emphasized the historic importance of the reinvestment of earnings to the expansion of American industry, but little attempt was made to show the

20 One contemporary study pointed out the possible advantage of holding company organizations in reducing the surtax on undistributed profits. *Facing the Tax Problem*, *op. cit.*, p. 180. Nevertheless, many instances are cited where subsidiaries were eliminated for the apparent purpose of reducing taxes (*ibid.*, p. 547).

21 *Message from the President*, *loc. cit.*

influence of tax policy on this development. The only significant statement in this respect was made by Owen D. Young, president of the General Electric Company, who remarked that the surtax was a matter of no consequence at all to his company which had reached a certain maturity of growth. He expressed some apprehension, however, over the possible restriction on the growth of new industries in which investors were hesitant to embark their savings.[22]

In its statistical investigation of the effects of tax policy, the T. N. E. C. devoted considerable attention to the undistributed profits tax. On the basis of available data supplied by the Treasury Department, one basic study concluded that, "In the case of growing or medium sized corporations which may not possess easy access to the capital market and therefore distribute less profits, it is not unlikely that an undistributed profits tax may operate to check 'monopolistic tendencies'."[23] Apparently no consideration was given to the more serious effects of the tax in those cases where reinvestment of profits was discouraged. It was conceded that the operation of the surtax did not curb existing monopolies.[24]

Other investigations have all supported the general belief that the taxation of retained earnings placed an undue handicap on the expansion of smaller companies. One influential report concluded that, "Its fundamental weakness is that it limits the possibility of prompt and flexible capital developments and handicaps with particular severity a multitude of small and medium sized business enterprises. It bears with particular severity upon new companies or those which are endeavoring to recuperate from a period of misfortune."[25]

22 Temporary National Economic Committee, *Hearings*, Part 9, pp. 3615-3622.

23 Clifford J. Hynning, *Taxation of Corporate Enterprise*, T.N.E.C. Monograph No. 9 (Washington, D. C., 1941), p. 89.

24 *Idem.*

25 M. Slade Kendrick, *op. cit.*, p. 92.

More recently a study of the effects of federal taxes on business incentives and income available for reinvestment emphasized the imperfections of the capital market in supplying corporate funds to growing industry and the potential loss to expansion represented by the drain of direct taxes on corporation income.[26] While no attention was devoted to the taxation of undistributed profits as such, it is clearly evident that the seriousness of the situation would be accentuated by such a policy, according to the view of the authors.

The conclusions presented above confirm the generally accepted opinion that the undistributed profits tax tended to promote the existing concentration in the control of industry. By discouraging the reinvestment of corporation earnings it deterred the growth of companies which, given adequate capital, would tend to resist the growing monopolistic influences of large, well established corporations. While companies with small earnings experienced less hardship under the law than is commonly supposed (as indicated by the substantial earnings they were able to retain at a preferential tax rate), the limitations imposed on the opportunity of more moderate size business to expand tended to strengthen the monopoly power of big business. Sale of new stock by use of preferential subscriptions does not appear to have been a practicable solution to the capital problems of intermediate size corporations requiring funds for growth.[27]

26 J. Keith Butters and John Lintner, *Effects of Federal Taxes on Growing Enterprises*, Harvard University, 1945, *passim*.

27 *Supra*, pp. 139-141.

CHAPTER VIII

THE EFFECT ON ECONOMIC STABILITY

1. Introduction

As the name itself implies, the tax on undistributed profits impinged on savings rather than consumption. Because of its effect on the distribution of corporation income, however, the reduction in savings greatly exceeded the income diverted to the public fisc in tax revenues. The new direction thereby given to the flow of incomes had important implications for the economy at large which transcended the effect of the surtax on the corporation itself.

It is the purpose of the following discussion to analyze the probable long-run influence of the corporation surtax on the expansion of the economy and to explore its possible reaction on the short term business cycle. While it is possible conceptually to distinguish between these phenomena, it is not always practicable to dissociate the two in practice. Moreover, since the experience of the tax was limited to the peak years of the unusually long business cycle of 1932 to 1938, it is not possible to trace its full effect over even a typical cycle (of approximately forty months).

Any analysis which ignores alternative sources of equivalent tax revenue provides only a partial answer. The undistributed profits tax is, therefore, compared to both the processing tax on agricultural commodities, which it replaced, and to an increase in the normal tax on corporation income, which succeeded it. The latter alternative was frequently advocated by spokesmen for business in consideration of the repeal of the surtax. The Revenue Act of 1938 increased the standard corporation rate from 15 to 19 per cent, but retained a remnant of the former dividend credit which permitted a maximum reduction in corporation taxes of two and one-half percentage points.

2. Long-Run Equilibrium

THE RELATIONSHIP OF SAVINGS TO INVESTMENT

The period of the 1930's evidenced a secular decline in the rate of growth of the economy which entailed an unprecedented amount of unemployment and maladjustment. Failure of private investment to recover necessitated investment-creating activities and other measures of the government in an effort to stimulate the full employment of resources. While the government policies were charged with impeding the full development of private enterprise, it is doubtful if business itself could have overcome the forces which tended to depress the economy. Highly progressive taxes, for example, were charged with discouraging business incentives, but the concatenation of technological, economic and social forces themselves appeared to diminish the investment opportunities available: The dearth of new technological developments, slacking rate of growth of population, expiration of a long-cycle building boom, and other factors all contributed to the declining secular rate of growth in national income.

Many believe that American business had bogged down in an inherent tendency of savings to exceed investment. It is generally recognized that the United States is a high savings economy as a result of its high concentration of incomes and institutional patterns of saving. Failure of the economy readily to absorb these savings by an equivalent increase in investment probably tended to stall the full development of resources during this period.[1]

The tendency toward under-investment was evidenced by many developments, among the most important being the following: (1) *Declining interest rates.* The steady decline in the interest rates on long-term corporation Aaa bonds, U. S. Government and municipal bonds during the period attest the

1 See, for example, Testimony of Alvin H. Hansen before the Temporary National Economic Committee, *Hearings*, Part 9, pp. 3495-3559.

relative abundance of funds seeking investment, compared to their demand. The yield on corporation bonds, for example, averaged 3.24 per cent in 1936 and 3.26 per cent in 1937 compared to 4.73 per cent in 1929. By 1939 corporation bond yields had dropped to 3.01 per cent.[2] (2) *Undue accumulation of cash by investment institutions.* Life insurance companies constitute the largest class of savings institutions, holding 42 per cent of such savings in 1938.[3] Cash holdings of the 26 largest companies alone increased by more than $500,000,000 between 1929 and 1938;[4] between 1938 and 1940 a further increase of 40 per cent was experienced. All insurance executives questioned by the Temporary National Economic Committee agreed that cash balances greatly exceeded business requirements because of the inability to find suitable investment outlets.[5] (3) *Accumulation of money "hoards" in general.* The failure of savings to flow into investment was evidenced by an accumulation of idle money of which the uninvested funds of insurance companies comprised only a part. The measurement of such "hoards," however, is complicated by the fact that they are not segregated in idle pools but manifested in a slackening velocity of money. On the assumption of a normal stable relationship between the quantity of money and the size of the national income (i.e., circular velocity) for different secular periods, one authority has shown that the size of money "hoards" increased progressively during the period of the 1930's to approximately twice the level of the late 1920's by 1936 and 1937.[6]

2 Computed by Moody's Investors Service, taken from *Statistical Abstract of the U. S.*

3 *Savings, Investment, and National Income*, T.N.E.C. Monograph No. 37, Washington, 1941, p. 35.

4 *Ibid.*, p. 44.

5 *Idem.*

6 James W. Angell, *Investment and Business Cycles* (New York: McGraw-Hill, 1941), p. 338. These estimates take into account an assumed secular decline in circular velocity from 1934 to 1940.

Uninterrupted expenditure of the income stream on consumption and investment goods is a necessary condition for the efficient functioning of the economy. Failure of investment to absorb the planned savings of the community will result in their dissipation in idle hoards and final waste through lack of employment in productive use. An economy geared to a high rate of savings, such as that of the United States, will continue to expand only so long as opportunities exist for their expenditure in equivalent investment, both public and private. Unless the proportion of savings is adjusted to the changing rate of secular growth in capital formation, therefore, the continued development of the economy is impeded by the failure of consumption to keep pace with the capacity of industry to produce. This appears to have been the situation during the decade of the 1930's. High concentration of incomes, inequalities in the distribution of wealth, institutional habits of saving for insurance, the heavy incidence of taxes on consumption, and other factors all combined to stall the economic machine whose requirements for capital formation had gone into low gear. To the extent that a secular decline had taken place in new investment opportunities, sustained economic development could be achieved primarily by a reduction in the proportion of national income saved and a larger share spent for consumption.

EFFECT OF THE CORPORATION SURTAX ON SAVING

The soundness of the undistributed profits tax policy should thus be appraised from the point of view of the economy as a whole with respect to its achievement of a better balance between savings and investment. It is essential first to isolate the quantitative changes in savings and consumption to which the tax contributed and then analyze the possible net effect of such changes on investment and expansion of the economy.

It was estimated above (page 33) that the undistributed profits tax compelled the distribution of approximately $1.1 billion that might otherwise have been retained by corporations in each of the years 1936 and 1937. In addition, the surtax is believed to have contributed to increased disbursements for wages, salaries, and other expenses of an indeterminate amount (see pp. 50-53). For lack of data on such bonuses, wage and salary increases, and other expenditures, these are assumed to be about $150,000,000 for each year. Thus, the total increase in corporation disbursements attributable to the corporation surtax (other than the surtax paid) is estimated roughly at $1.25 billion. Of this amount it is estimated that approximately $250,000,000 was collected by the Federal government alone in income taxes, leaving roughly $1.0 billion disposable income in the hands of individuals, partnerships, trusts and tax exempt institutions.[7]

Of the approximately $1.0 billion in disposable income remaining in each of these years, it is estimated that about one half, or $500 million was saved and $500 million spent on consumption goods. This allocation is based essentially on sample data of the proportion of net income saved at various income levels.[8] These estimates were revised upward, however, to take account of the unusual circumstances of the increase in

7 In 1936 only $3,946 million out of total net dividend payments of $4,793 million reported by corporations was declared to the Treasury Department, including $718 million received by fiduciaries. The balance of $757 million, or 16 per cent, was presumably received by individuals not filing returns, partnerships, and tax exempt corporations. A large part, no doubt, represented evasion. (*Bulletin of the Treasury Department*, January, 1943, p. 4.) The proportions for 1937 are similar. In estimating tax revenue, the net increase of $1.1 billion in dividends was apportioned by income class in accordance with the distribution of all dividends reported by individuals and fiduciaries (after allowance for 16 per cent unclassified), and the marginal surtax rates applied. The estimate of $225 million in tax revenue from dividend income agrees roughly with preliminary estimates of the Treasury Department of $230 to $250 million. (*Hearings, Committee on Ways and Means, Revenue Revision Act*, 1938, p. 149). An amount of $25 million was added to take account of other increased income attributed to the tax, including $50-60 million of taxable stock dividends not included in the estimates of corporation income distributed.

8 *Consumer Expenditures in the United States, 1935-1936.* National Resources Committee, Washington, 1939, Table 8, p. 48.

dividend income. Additional allowances were made for retention by fiduciaries and the amount recouped directly by corporations through the extensive use of quasi-coercive stock rights, which otherwise might not have been saved and reinvested. Account was also taken of the probable increase in individual savings attributed to the fact that corporation savings were reduced.[9]

It seems clear that the taxation of undistributed profits was calculated to effect the greatest reduction in the proportion of the national income saved of any alternative tax policy. Not only did the surtax paid by the corporation itself impinge directly on corporation savings, but the effect of the surtax was to stimulate the distribution of corporation earnings which otherwise would have been saved. All together, about $1.4 billion a year, including the surtax liability, was distributed.[10] Of this amount an estimated $0.5 billion was saved by individuals and others, leaving a net reduction in savings of the community of approximately $0.9 billion.

If the equivalent amount of revenue were raised by an increase in the corporation normal tax, the reduction in savings would have approximated only $0.4 billion. Thus, an increase in consumer purchasing power of about $0.5 billion yearly can be attributed to the taxation of undistributed profits ($0.9 billion less $0.4 billion tax revenue). Contrasted with the processing tax, however, which the new tax replaced, the stimulus to purchasing power can be measured by almost the full amount of the reduction in savings estimated above, $0.9 billion. While the incidence of the processing tax rested in part on the producers (and to a minor extent on processors), the tax

9 Paul Samuelson has estimated that an increase in business savings of of $1.00 results in an increase in consumption by stockholders of roughly 23 cents. A. H. Hansen, *Fiscal Policy and Business Cycles* (New York: W. W. Norton & Co., Inc., 1941), p. 259.

10 In 1936 the surtax liability was $145 million, and in 1937, $176 million (*Statistics of Income for 1936 and 1937*) which added to the $1.25 billion dividends and other income attributed to the tax gives a yearly average of about $1.4 billion.

was shifted very substantially to consumers in higher prices of farm products.[11]

In these respects the taxation of undistributed profits tended to bring about a more desirable balance in the proportions of the national income saved and spent on consumer goods. Whether it contributed to a better equilibrium between savings and investment remains to be explored. First, however, it is necessary to examine the internal sources of corporation investment in order to determine the relative importance of reinvested earnings to the gross savings available from all sources.

THE IMPACT ON CORPORATION GROSS SAVINGS

Retained profits account for only a portion of the internal funds available to the corporation for reinvestment. Substantial contributions are also made from depletion and depreciation allowances which, of course, were relatively unaffected by the surtax on undistributed profits. The importance of such savings to the total gross savings of corporations earning net income is indicated by Table No. 20. Here it is seen that depreciation and depletion allowances have supplied a rather steady stream of savings to net income companies, whose relative importance has varied with the size of net profits available for distribution. The average proportion of internal funds supplied from these sources during the two years before and after the biennium of the undistributed profits tax was about 61.0 per cent, compared to about 69.0 per cent supplied in the surtax years themselves. In other words, 39.0 per cent of gross corporation savings was derived on the average from retained profits under " normal " conditions, contrasted with 31.0 per cent remaining after the tax on undistributed profits.

While represented by depreciation and depletion charges on the books of the corporation, these charges make available

11 *An Analysis of the Effects of the Processing Taxes Levied Under the Agricultural Adjustment Act*, prepared by the U. S. Department of Agriculture. U. S. Treasury Department, Washington, 1937, pp. 6, 7.

to the corporation an equivalent amount of funds (less whatever operating deficit is incurred). The utilization of such

TABLE NO. 20

NEW CAPITAL ISSUES AND GROSS SAVINGS BY ALL NET INCOME CORPORATIONS, 1934-1940

(Millions of dollars)

	New capital issues (Long term)	Corporation savings			
		Depreciation allowances	Depletion allowances	Undistributed profits	Total
1934 ..	$ 146	$1,721	$152	$ 965	$2,838
1935 ..	393	1,905	179	1,375	3,459
1936 ..	1,170	2,342	332	1,235	3,909
1937 ..	1,178	2,396	395	1,262	4,053
1938 ..	870	2,051	261	1,200	3,512
1939 ..	379	2,491	300	2,212	5,003
1940 ..	724	2,801	373	2,906	6,080

Source: New Capital issues derived from *Commercial and Financial Chronicle* Series, *Statistical Abstract of the United States;* Corporation Savings: *Statistics of Income,* Part 2.

funds is at the discretion of management, and while expressly provided for the purpose of maintaining capital intact, they may, of course, be used currently for a variety of needs such as working capital, liquidation of liabilities, investment in plant and equipment, and even payment of dividends. In these respects their application to business purposes is indistinguishable from the use of retained profits. Expenditure of depreciation allowances may thus be currently made to enlarge plant capacity. Pending actual retirement of the assets depreciated, the maximum net expansion thereby provided may be substantial, and is indicated by the size of the depreciation reserves shown on the corporation books.[12]

According to the Bureau of Internal Revenue statistics (Table No. 20), the gross savings of all net income corporations (i.e., those affected by the surtax) averaged about $4.0

12 Allowances should, of course, be made for the decline in productivity, due to wear and tear, inadequacy, and obsolescence of the old assets still retained in use. On the other hand, technological improvements contributed to a greater productivity of a given amount of investment, compared with past periods.

billion in the years 1936 and 1937. If it is considered that the profits retained by net income companies in these years were reduced by about $1.25 billion, as a result of the surtax (other than the amount of surtax paid), gross savings would have amounted to about $5.25 billion. The net reduction of internal funds available for reinvestment (and other purposes) was, therefore, approximately 20 per cent.

EFFECT ON INVESTMENT

The question is properly raised as to whether the net reduction in yearly savings available to the community (and corporations) contributed to a better equilibrium with new investment. If the reduction in savings were offset by an equivalent curtailment of public or private investment, the tendency to oversave would have remained unaffected. While the proportion of savings to the national income would have been reduced, the amount of new capital formation would have likewise suffered.

A priori, opportunities for new investment should not have been impaired by the surtax. If the rate of growth in innovations and new industries requiring large amounts of capital had undergone a secular decline, the availability of internal savings itself would not have generated any new demand (except indirectly in their employment in research and development). On the other hand, the expenditure of dividend income should have improved the profit prospects of consumption goods industries, raised the level of business expectations generally, and ultimately contributed to an expansion of plant capacity through new investment. Should this be the case, the increased expenditure of corporation income on consumer goods induced by the surtax should have enhanced business investment rather than impeded it.

The exploitation of investment opportunities also depends on the relative availability and cost of capital. In this respect undistributed earnings are generally regarded as "costless" funds to the corporation and, therefore, provide a substantial source of "venture" capital for the development of new products and promotion of new business which would otherwise tend to be neglected.[13] While their reinvestment may in principle be justified only in terms of their "opportunity cost," as measured by their prospective rate of return in other enterprises with a similar degree of risk, it is questionable if management is actually guided by such fine considerations.[14] The price imposed on the retention of earnings by the surtax, therefore, undoubtedly deterred some investment which might otherwise have been undertaken. Of this effect there is considerable evidence.[15] The alternative cost of financing such expansion by sale of bonds and stock as well as the inability of many small and medium size businesses to secure such capital, tended to discourage industry from carrying out expansion plans.

So far as corporations were concerned, however, it is clear that the drain of funds attributed to the surtax was not accompanied by an equivalent loss in investment. Substantial amounts were recouped by the use of quasi-coercive stock rights in the sale of new capital stock and convertible bonds to shareholders (see pp. 118-130). In lieu of business savings, external funds were secured by public sale of bonds, preferred stock and other securities for the purpose of implementing expansion plans. Finally, the commercial banks supplied an appreciable amount of funds, on a short term and intermediate term basis, which otherwise would not have been necessitated. Internal sources of capital were thus replaced in large part by external financing in meeting the requirements for new investment.

While the financial policies of all corporations were adapted in varying degrees to the new conditions, it is likely that expan-

13 Together with other internal corporation savings derived from depreciation and depletion allowances they probably provide the bulk of such "venture" capital. See O. Altman, *op. cit.*, p. 58.

14 *Ibid.*, p. 91.

15 See, for example, the response to questionnaires presented by: M. Slade Kendrick, *op. cit.*, pp. 42, 43; W. L. Thorp and E. B. George, *loc. cit.*, p. 23; *Hearings before the Committee on Ways and Means*, Revenue Revision Laws, 1938, p. 777.

sion plans of larger corporations were interrupted less by the undistributed profits tax than those of smaller companies. Since large listed corporations account for the preponderance of new investment, the availability of such funds in the capital market is relevant to the success with which the expansion plans were carried out.

The fact that the sales of securities for new capital purposes in the years 1936 and 1937 greatly exceeded the amount in any other year of this period evidences the importance of the market supply of funds for new investment (see Table No. 20). But the question still remains of whether the sale of new issues would have reached the same proportions if the normal proportion of earnings had been retained. If judged by the situation in 1939 and 1940 when the national income was equal to or exceeded that of 1936 and 1937, the question would appear to be answered in the negative. During 1939 and 1940 new capital issues aggregated only $380,000,000 and $725,000,000,

TABLE NO. 21

SOURCES OF FUNDS OF 58 INDUSTRIAL COMPANIES, 1934-1939
(Millions of dollars)

	1934	1935	1936	1937	1938	1939
Net income	$233	549	902	1,077	420	713
Dividends paid	269	323	669	742	393	531
Undistributed profits	— 36	226	233	335	27	182
Depreciation	393	428	460	500	500	537
Common stock	—7	18	119	148	4	7
Preferred stock	—1	—33	—5	52	—1	0
Long term debt	—114	—66	—21	—10	324	42
Short term liabilities	88	177	236	156	—299	180
Residual	— 9	—14	21	19	— 9	—58
Total	$314	736	1,043	1,200	546	890

Source: Compiled by Division of Research and Statistics, Board of Governors of the Federal Reserve System. Taken from *Savings, Investment, and National Income*, T.N.E.C. Monograph No. 37, p. 121.

respectively, an amount appreciably below the $1.2 billion distributed in both 1936 and 1937.

Additional light is thrown on this question by the experience of 58 identical industrial corporations over the period of the undistributed profits tax as shown in Table No. 21.[16] One of the most striking features in the financing of these companies was the unusual increase in funds secured from external sources in 1936 and 1937. Capital stock issues amounted to $114 and $200 million, respectively, for these years, compared to very negligible amounts in the preceding and following years. There was a net reduction in long term borrowing but the increase in short term loans was very substantial. Because of the unusually large increase in profits during 1936 and 1937, it seems likely that the amount of earnings retained would have been substantially greater if the surtax had not encouraged their distribution, and that the corporations were driven to the capital market and banks in order to finance a substantial increase in investment during 1936 and 1937.

It is also significant that these corporations drew down considerable amounts of cash and marketable securities in 1936 and 1937 in order to provide funds for new investment. The importance of this source of funds is indicated by a comparison with other years when cash and marketable securities actually increased:[17]

Year	Change in cash and marketable securities (millions)
1934	$— 84
1935	36
1936	— 41
1937	—242
1938	367
1939	273

Thus new investment in the years of the undistributed profits tax actually exceeded the funds provided from other internal and external sources, as summarized in Table No. 21. To this extent, a reduction in " hoarding " was evidenced.

16 This sample includes 9 steel, 7 automobile, 11 petroleum, 18 machinery, 4 rubber and tire, and 7 tobacco companies whose total assets in 1936 amounted to $11.4 billion. *Savings and Investment*, Hearings before the T.N.E.C., Part 9, p. 4045.

17 *Ibid.*

The above data do not evidence any significant curtailment in investment which might be attributed to the undistributed profits tax. Because of the superior ability of these listed companies to tap the capital market and other sources of credit at a minimum of cost, it is unlikely that their expenditures on new investment were much if any less than otherwise. In other words, funds from the sale of securities, bank loans, and other sources probably replaced a substantial portion of earnings that would otherwise have remained undistributed. While the record may have been less favorable for small and medium size corporations, the magnitude of their investment is greatly exceeded by the large listed companies.[18]

3. Cyclical Effects

The effects of the undistributed profits tax on cyclical fluctuations is best examined against the backdrop of the particular economic and political forces which generated the business cycle with which it was associated. It is, therefore, desirable to review briefly the principal features of the unusually long business cycle which ran its course from the depths of the great depression in 1932 through its peak in mid-1937 and subsequent trough in 1938.

Despite the extraordinarily long recovery period, national income increased at the annual rate of about $5.0 billion per year between 1932 and 1937. This expansion tapered off by

18 In 1937 there were 1,961 corporations whose securities were listed on organized securities exchanges. Excluding industry groups not registered with the S. E. C., these represented about three and one-half per cent of the number of all American corporations but are estimated to account for about 60 per cent of corporation assets reported to the Bureau of Internal Revenue. *Statistics of American Listed Corporations, Part I.* From data collected by the *Survey of American Listed Corporations*, a W. P. A. study sponsored by the S. E. C. (December, 1940), p. 6. Inclusion of industry groups not required to register with the S. E. C., such as railroads, communications, insurance, banks and trust companies and investment trusts, would probably increase the coverage of listed companies to somewhat more than 60 per cent. Account should also be taken of those companies whose securities are traded over-the-counter.

May, 1937, and turned into one of the most precipitous declines in recent business annals. Much has been written about the underlying causes of the failure of business to attain the level of 1929, but even this level of production would have left a large residue of unemployment because of the increase in population during this period. Among the many factors held responsible was the undistributed profits tax itself which coincided with the peak and downturn of this cycle.

For those who look for an explanation in particular circumstances, attention should be directed to the multitude of special conditions which contributed to the recovery and characterized its peak. Among the most important of these were the self-generating factors which largely account for any business recovery: The accumulated backlog of deferred demand on the one hand, and the deterioration of business assets on the other, which necessitated unusually large expenditures of funds for the rehabilitation of plant and equipment. In addition, considerable modernization was dictated by the recent technological improvements in production, of which the continuous strip steel mill is a notable instance. In 1937 expenditures on plant equipment and related producers goods actually approached those of 1929 (at 1929 prices) as shown by the following comparison:

	(Billions of dollars) 1929	1937 (1929 prices)
New construction		
Business	$ 4.2	$ 1.7
Residential	3.7	1.9
Public	2.4	2.1
Net change in inventories	2.4	2.6
Net change in foreign claims	0.4	—0.1
Producers goods	7.5	6.6
Total	$20.6	$14.8

Source: Simon Kuznets, *National Product Since 1869*. National Bureau of Economic Research (1946). Derived from Tables, Part I.

Many weaknesses were evident, however, as compared to the structure of gross capital formation of 1929. Business expenditures on plant reached less than half the volume of 1929 expenditures; private housing construction also failed to exceed the same half-way mark. Perhaps the most significant evidence of the precarious basis of the boom, however, was the fact that it rested disproportionately on investment in inventories: The change in value of inventories that took place in 1937 was the only category in which 1929 investment was exceeded.

Governmental policy strongly influenced the course of the cycle. While the Federal government had contributed substantially to the recovery by its pump-priming program of deficit financing, by 1937 the net contribution of government to investment (including state and local) had rapidly tapered off from $366 million in December, 1936 to only $37 million in March, 1937. The total volume of deficit spending in 1937 was only $806 million compared to over $4,000 million in 1936.[19] This curtailment was signaled by a presidential announcement of a sharp reduction in public works. Stimulus of the veterans' bonus expenditures of over half a billion dollars which began in 1936 had probably also worked off by the middle of 1937. Meanwhile the Federal Reserve Board, apprehensive of an incipient runaway situation, put a damper on business expectations by successive increases in the reserve requirements in August, 1936 and in March and May, 1937, to double the previous ratio.

By the middle of 1937, then, the business up-turn appeared to have run its course. Fundamentally it seems clear that the expansion rested on a rather unsubstantial economic basis which foreshadowed the impending collapse. Weaknesses were evident from the failure of private construction to recover as well as in the undue accumulation of inventories. When the net contribution of the Federal deficit spending was curtailed, the props which largely sustained the recovery were withdrawn; the premature action of the Federal Reserve Board

19 Henry H. Villard, *Deficit Spending and the National Income* (New York: Farrar & Rinehart, 1941), p. 323.

probably only hastened the onset of the recession which lasted until the last quarter of 1938.

THE CONDITIONS OF STABILITY

The short term business cycle is characterized by greater fluctuations in the production of producers goods (and durable consumption goods) than in the production of consumer goods in general. Briefly, the explanation of an upward movement appears to be found in the intensified effect of a given (or anticipated) change in consumers' purchases on the expenditures for producers goods necessary to satisfy consumption demand. Producers' expenditures generate more consumption demand and the fluctuations become self-multiplying in character. If producers' expenditures were limited to the real savings of the community in the first instance, the effect of increased expenditures would be self-limiting and the violence of the fluctuations would be mitigated. That is, offsets in available savings would tend to limit the multiplying effect of a given increase in expenditure on producers goods.

One of the essential factors contributing to the stability of business appears to be a high correlation of savings with changes in the national income. If the rate of increase in investment during the expansion phase is accompanied by a high rate of decline in the marginal propensity to consume (or increasing marginal propensity to save) the multiplier effect of a given change in investment on general employment and prices tends to be limited.[20] Excessive expansion is thereby curbed and the severity of the ensuing recession correspondingly ameliorated.

The American economy has normally been characterized by a high sensitivity of savings to changes in national income. Offsets to increased investment are more or less automatically entailed in the savings provided by the profits generated in

20 See J. M. Keynes, *The General Theory of Employment, Interest and Money* (New York: Harcourt, Brace and Co., 1936), p. 250.

business expansion itself. Dividend distributions, in fact, largely account for the high concentration of incomes from which a major portion of American savings is derived. The average percentage of dividend income increases with the size of individual incomes. Figures for 1936 show that on the average 25 per cent of the difference between a gross income of $5,000 and $10,000 was accounted for by dividend receipts; 50 per cent of the difference between a gross income of $25,000 and $50,000, and 75 per cent of the difference between an income of $500,000 and $1,000,000 were likewise attributed to dividend income alone.[21] Since the percentage of income saved increases with its size, the major indirect contribution of business profits to savings is readily apparent. The corporation is responsible more directly, however, for the most significant contribution to national savings. Including gross savings of corporations derived from depreciation allowances as well as retained net profits, the marginal propensity to save by American corporations was demonstrated to be as high as 49 per cent over a long period of years.[22] Directly and indirectly, then, it is apparent that savings are geared to fluctuations in business profits and a basic stabilizing factor thereby supplied to the business cycle.

The manner in which the undistributed profits tax altered the institutional pattern of savings has already been illustrated (pp. 153-154). With reference to the peak years of the business cycle of 1933 to 1938, it was estimated that, including the corporation surtax, corporations disbursed annually in the neighborhood of $1.4 billion that might otherwise have been retained and reinvested. Of this amount an estimated $0.5 billion was saved by individuals. The net reduction in savings, therefore,

21 Martin Taitel, *Profits, Productive Activities, and New Investment*, T.N.E.C. Monograph No. 12, p. 53.

22 Estimates of Paul Samuelson presented in Alvin H. Hansen, *Fiscal Policy and Business Cycles*, p. 255. Because of the high degree of intercorrelation among the factors employed, these estimates, while confirmed by other studies, are subject to a large margin of error.

was near $0.9 billion, which was diverted to the government by taxes ($0.4 billion) and to consumption ($0.5 billion). The resulting increase in consumer purchasing power probably stimulated further investment in capital goods and inventories (as well as purchases of durable consumers goods) which tended to be financed by an expansion of bank credit. It seems clear, then, that the taxation of undistributed profits tended to impair the resistence of the economy to cyclical change.[23] Because of this tendency, one economist stated, "The real objection to undistributed profits taxation may be found less in the fact that it constitutes a hindrance to the financing of small business than in the fact that it would tend to increase the violence of cyclical fluctuations."[24]

Alternative sources of an equivalent amount of tax revenue should be considered, however, in appraising the net effect of the tax on savings. As a replacement of the processing tax, whose incidence rested largely on consumption rather than savings, the above estimate is probably not unrealistic. As a

23 Because of the unsettled and controversial status of business cycle theory, most studies of the undistributed profits tax have simply indicated the opposing points of view and let the reader take his choice. One such study presents (but does not necessarily endorse) the argument that the severity of booms and depressions would be decreased, ". . . since a brake would be put on excessive expansion." (*Facing the Tax Problem, op. cit.*, p. 470). Others point out that a reduction was made in the most unstable part of the economy, *i.e.*, investment. Any decrease in investment which may have occurred probably left open certain investment opportunities to cushion the following recession and enable a quicker recovery. See, for example, John R. Hicks, *Value and Capital* (London: Oxford University Press, 1939), p. 298. J. M. Clark suggests that we should spend more and save less than we do at the height of a boom in order to better maintain stability. *Strategic Factors in Business Cycles.* (New York: National Bureau of Economic Research, 1934), p. 153. But he immediately raises the question of whether the increased demand would not stimulate still further the concentrated production of capital goods financed by credit expansion. The latter result he believes more probable. (*Ibid.*, p. 154).

24 Moses Abramovitz, "Savings and Investments: Profits vs. Prosperity?", *American Economic Review Supplement*, Vol. XXXII, No. 2, Part 2. June, 1942, p. 69.

substitute for a direct increase in the corporation normal tax, the differential would have been reduced in all liklihood only by the estimated amount of tax revenues, $400,000,000, thus contributing to a net decline in savings of a like amount rather than $900,000,000.

THE ROLE OF BANK CREDIT

Business expansion is facilitated by the creation of bank credit which supplies the means of increasing business expenditures for which funds are unavailable from other sources. Bank loans and investments, therefore, probably replaced in large part the drain of corporation funds which would have been retained, but for the corporation surtax, to finance working capital requirements. The inflationary influences of the undistributed profits tax can thus be measured largely by the extent to which bank credit was substituted for business savings.[25]

It is obviously impossible to isolate the expansion of bank credit induced by the reduction in corporation savings.[26] It is, nevertheless, significant that bank loans and investments did expand appreciably over the years 1936 and 1937, thereby lending some circumstantial evidence to the hypothesis presented above. The expansion of loans and investments of all insured banks from the beginning of 1936 to the middle of 1937 is presented as follows: [27]

25 This is a highly oversimplified statement which ignores the changes taking place in the utilization of money, i. e., its income velocity. However, since the average income velocity remained virtually unchanged over the period of the study, the hypothesis is substantially correct.

26 One survey disclosed that 42 per cent of the respondents resorted to the use of bank loans that would not have been necessary except for the tax on undistributed profits; many companies reported this to be their first use of bank credit. Revenue Revision of 1938, *Hearings before the Committee on Ways and Means*, p. 777.

27 Source: Federal Deposit Insurance Corporation, biennial reports.

	December 31, 1935	June 30, 1937	Increase
		(Millions of dollars)	
Obligations of the U. S. ..	$13,275.2	$13,964.7	$ 689.5
Other securities	6,841.1	7,213.9	372.8
Loans and discounts	14,698.0	17,014.6	2,316.6
Total	$34,814.3	$38,193.2	$3,378.9

Total bank loans and investments increased $3.4 billion over the peak of the business cycle covered by the undistributed profits tax. About 70 per cent of the increase was accounted for by loans and discounts to business, which expanded 15 per cent over the period of 18 months. The relevance of this expansion in business loans to the pressing credit requirements of business is perhaps best exemplified, however, by the accelerated increase in loans and discounts that took place in successive periods of the cycle, up to the peak of June 30, 1937:[28]

Period	Increase in loans and discounts
June 30, 1935 to Dec. 30, 1935	$ 188.0
Dec. 31, 1935 to June 30, 1936	409.2
June 30, 1936 to Dec. 31, 1936	832.5
Dec. 31, 1936 to June 30, 1937	1,074.9

These figures indicate the cumulative inflationary influences at work during the climax of the cycle, which was brought to a sudden stop around August of 1937. By the end of the year 1937, loans and discounts experienced a net liquidation of about $300 million from the middle of the year.

The trend of investments in " other securities " is equally interesting. While bank portfolios undoubtedly included a substantial amount of tax-exempt municipal and state bonds, investments in corporation securities were also prominent. Investments in other securities expanded most rapidly during the first six months of 1936 when $570 million were acquired. They continued to increase toward the end of the year by an additional $146 million, and then declined $345 million between

28 *Ibid.*

then and June, 1937. By the end of 1937, the total amount had dropped to the level of the beginning of the period, January 1, 1936. Thus, the net expansion in business credit during the two-year period under review was accounted for almost wholly by bank loans and discounts, a large portion of which undoubtedly included term loans of an intermediate maturity, from two to ten years.

The large volume of loans and investments to business during 1936 and 1937 substantiates the view that banks were not, in fact, deterred by the surtax from supplying the legitimate credit requirements of business. They provided an alternative source of funds to which business, both large and small, had more or less ready access in meeting the drain on business savings attributed to the undistributed profits tax itself.

The rapid increase in bank credit over this period illustrates the inflationary influences to which the surtax undoubtedly contributed. Whether the contribution was significant or not, it is impossible to determine.

EFFECT ON CORPORATION RESERVES

The influence of the surtax on cyclical instability may also be examined from the point of view of the corporation. Much of the criticism of the surtax centered on its effect in impairing corporation reserves, which were alleged to provide a factor of stability or " cushion " against the vicissitudes of business. While the " cushion " argument has some validity in practice it is believed that its real effect has either been largely misunderstood or distorted by ambiguous and exaggerated claims.

Unless the corporation retains out of current earnings a fund of idle cash or investments in highly liquid securities such as government bonds, no reserve in the real sense of the word exists. Such " reserves " as are ordinarily established by corporations are identified by nothing more than the earmarking of the earned surplus account, for special or general purposes. Such practice, whether indicated formally or not, has the effect of establishing a bench mark or limit below which surplus is considered to be unavailable for dividend distribution, but does not in itself alter in any respect the composition of the assets of the corporation; these may, in fact, be heavily invested in fixed plant and equipment, inventories, and accounts receivable, with no more than the normal amount of cash essential to the conduct of business. While retained profits have been employed to increase cash, particularly during periods of business depression when liquidity preferences are high, it is believed that this has been true only to a limited extent. The more likely disposition of retained earnings is either to increase investment in other current or fixed assets, or to extinguish short term and long term liabilities. In many cases preferred and common stock are retired with these funds.

To the extent that corporation earnings realized in cash are utilized for the liquidation of bank loans and funded debt, the corporation does indeed increase its financial strength and its power to meet an emergency. It may generally be concluded, therefore, that the risk of failure and possibly bankruptcy and liquidation is avoided to the extent that equity capital is employed as a buffer against adversity. While the undistributed profits tax did not preclude the maintenance of such a "cushion," the pressure of the tax did undoubtedly lead to some unwise and imprudent distributions.

It may be contended that the sale of stock for purposes of working capital is equally effective in maintaining the equity position of a corporation. Such policy was, in fact, followed by many large corporations. But the same opportunity was not open to all, particularly small and medium companies without access to the capital market, or by any corporation when market conditions were not favorable for sale of equity securities. Such a situation would be particularly true during a business recession when the need for such capital may be urgent.

It is also contended that the undistributed profits tax militated against the maintenance of purchasing power during a depression by discouraging regularity in dividend payments and maintenance of salaries and wages. The validity of this argument, of course, depends on whether or not earnings of profitable years can be reinvested and later drawn upon for business purposes during a depression. While its importance is probably greatly exaggerated, the possibility remains of providing such funds through liquidation of current assets and, to some extent, fixed assets. Such funds are commonly employed first to extinguish short term bank loans and other liabilities. Bank credit is thereby deflated and no income creating disbursement is realized. Funds may also be made available from the liquidation of assets for payment of dividends and maintenance of salaries and wages. In this respect, a useful purpose is served in maintaining purchasing power and tempering the severity of the depresion. It may, therefore, be reasoned that to the extent bank loans were necessitated by the distribution of earnings that would have otherwise been retained, funds were unavailable for maintenance of purchasing power during a recession. In this respect the undistributed profits tax might have accentuated the severity of a business decline.

The importance of dividend and wage stabilization, however, can easily be exaggerated. It is not possible to determine the extent to which either contribute to the alleviation of business depressions, but certainly they must have been insignificant against the deflationary forces of the great depression following 1929. On the other hand, the business recession of 1938, following upon the undistributed profits tax itself, could not be characterized as unduly severe. While major in amplitude, its duration was relatively short. Moreover, dividend payments in 1938 were no less than could be expected from the normal relationship between earnings and their distribution (Table No. 3, p. 34). Since each business cycle is unique, it is not possible to generalize from the experience of one. Had the undistributed profits tax remained in effect, the psychological irritant it represented to business might have forestalled an early recovery from the trough of 1938.

One thorough study of corporation policy during the early part of the depression with respect to dividend payments raised serious doubts whether corporate reserves assure wage and dividend payments during poor years.[29] In fact, the possibility was presented " . . . that a period of disinvesting, dishoarding, and real capital liquidation made possible by surplus accumulation may result in less employment of all factors of production during recession periods and hence the payment of less wages and dividends."[30] The following additional pertinent observations were made with respect to dividend policy in practice:

" 2. Depression dividends were paid by companies that continued to operate profitably, and only limited amounts were paid in excess of earnings. Very moderate dividends were paid by companies reporting losses, with few outstanding exceptions.

" 4. The corporations that found it necessary to charge dividends to surplus made drastic reductions in dividend rates and although the aggregate amount of dividends paid from surplus is large in a number of cases, these payments are small when compared with earnings withheld during the twenties.

" 5. There is no apparent relationship between earnings reinvested during the twenties and dividends paid during the early thirties."[31]

Conclusion

If it is granted that the corporation surtax did, in fact, contribute an element of instability to the short business cycle (an effect which can by no means be " proved ") the same influence can be attributed, though with less force, to all taxes on corporation income and highly progressive taxes on individual incomes. But this untoward effect does not necessarily in itself

29 O. J. Curry, *Utilization of Corporate Profits in Prosperity and Depression*, Michigan Business Studies, Vol. IX, No. 4, Ann Arbor, Michigan (1941), p. 92.

30 *Idem.*

31 *Ibid.*, p. 93.

alter the desirability of such taxes, even assuming they cannot be shifted. If it can be demonstrated equally well that the same forces tend to enhance the long run level of the economy by raising the *average* propensity to consume and thereby curbing the institutional tendency toward over-savings which is accounted for so largely by corporation profits, the choice would be clearly in favor of the taxation of undistributed income. It is still a moot question, however, of whether the American economy has, indeed, matured to the point where innovations and opportunities for investment are less than the proportions which marked its progress over the last century or so of the new industrial revolution. One analysis undertaken during the period of the tax concluded that, "In the long run . . . it appears to be true that a system with progressive rates of income and inheritance taxes, and with some checks on self-financing may contribute to the achievement of a better balanced economic order." [32] This view still appears to be valid even considering the surge of investment now in prospect for several years to come.

32 Gerhard Colm and Fritz Lehman, *Economic Consequences of Recent American Tax Policy*, Supplement 1, Social Research (1938), p. 71.

CHAPTER IX

SUMMARY AND CONCLUSIONS

1. Historical

The coordination of income taxes on corporations and individuals has presented a major problem to the Federal government since enactment of the first modern income tax in 1913. The corporation income tax was apparently first designed for the collection of personal income taxes at the source, for which a tax credit was allowed individuals on dividends received. This tax credit device was continued until 1935, but its equivalence with the corporation rate had long since disappeared with the revenue measures of the first World War. More significant, however, was the inherent disparity between the flat corporation rate and graduated surtax rates on individual income. The opportunity for avoidance of higher personal income taxes through the retention of corporation earnings provided one of the most serious inequities in the Federal tax system.

Several attempts were made during the 1920's to correct the disparity between income taxes on individuals and corporations by enactment of a compensatory tax on undistributed profits, but they did not succeed in passing the Congress. The increased personal surtax rates enacted during the first Roosevelt administration greatly accentuated the differential between the two taxes and finally led to the advocacy of a tax on undistributed profits which would reduce the inequality. While the recommendation of President Roosevelt was precipitated by emergency needs for additional revenue to replace the processing taxes outlawed by the Supreme Court and to meet the advance payment of the veterans bonus, the taxation of retained income was regarded as a permanent reform of the income tax which was long overdue.

The taxation of undistributed profits was approved by the Congress against considerable opposition. While the principle was accepted, the final measure bore little resemblance to the original proposals of the Administration as incorporated in the House bill. Whereas the recommendation would have replaced all existing corporation taxes by a levy on net income graduated with the percentage of income retained, Congress enacted a graduated surtax on undistributed profits which supplemented the normal tax rate. The surtax on undistributed profits survived the years 1936 and 1937 as one of the most controversial tax measures ever enacted by an American legislature. It was effectively repealed by the Revenue Act of 1938 but a remnant remained for two more years in the form of a normal tax credit for dividends paid.

Considerable opposition can be expected against any radical change in tax laws, particularly one which impinged so sharply on the established practices of American business. In this respect one must concur with the observation of Canard that new taxes are bad because they upset the existing equilibria. The reaction on business of the undistributed profits tax far transcended its impact on the corporation as such; it had important effects on the entire economy which have never been fully determined. In retrospect, however, the effects of the undistributed profits tax do not appear to have been so serious as its most violent critics have charged, or so desirable as its most ardent proponents have claimed. While the principle of a compensatory tax on undistributed profits is believed to be both equitable and sound, the form in which it was enacted left a great deal to be desired in practice.

2. Impact on the Corporation

DISTRIBUTION OF CORPORATION EARNINGS

The surtax on undistributed profits resulted in a substantial increase in dividends. The net increase (after eliminating intercorporate dividends) is estimated at approximately $1.1 billion in each of the years 1936 and 1937. This amounted to approximately one third greater dividend income than would probably otherwise have been received by individuals, trusts and tax exempt institutions in each of these years.

Considerable variations were experienced by major industry groups with respect to the increase in dividends attributable to the surtax. The greatest increases were found in the construction industry and agriculture, forestry and fisheries group, whose dividend payments averaged about 75 per cent greater than they might otherwise have been. More modest increases were found in the transportation, real estate and service industries, averaging from 25 to 30 per cent. Neither the mining industry nor the public utility industry was noticably affected by the surtax. The largest contribution to the net increase in dividends was made, however, by the manufacturing and trade groups, which accounted for more than 80 per cent of the total increase in each of the undistributed profits tax years. The expansion in dividends was remarkably uniform in each of the two years, being about 40 per cent greater in the case of manufacturing and from 50 to 55 per cent greater in the case of trade companies.

In general, a greater compulsion was given to the distribution of earnings by small and medium size corporations than by the giant corporations, as measured by size of assets. (Since the percentage of earnings normally distributed varies directly with the size of the corporation, there was, of course, more margin for increase). On the other hand, the relative increase by giant corporations (with assets in excess of $50,000,000) was equal to the average for industry as a whole. Because of the high concentration of corporation profits in these companies, they were largely responsible for the greatly enhanced dividends of the period. The larger medium size companies increased dividends by less than the industry average.

The surtax on retained profits also stimulated the distributions of earnings more directly through increased wages, salaries, bonuses to employees and executives, as well as through higher expenses on advertising, maintenance and other items.

While it is impossible to measure the full effects of these expenditures attributable to the surtax, they are believed to have been rather general and substantial, particularly for smaller and medium size corporations. Larger executive salaries and bonuses enabled the owners of small businesses to reduce corporation normal taxes as well as to avoid the surtax.

ECONOMIC FACTORS INFLUENCING THE DISTRIBUTION OF EARNINGS

The increased distribution of earnings was, of course, motivated by the desire to avoid or to minimize income taxes. In the case of small and medium size companies there was a tendency to distribute earnings up to the point where the increase in taxes paid by the stockholders on their individual income was equal to the reduction in surtaxes on corporation income. Conflicts of interest among stockholders in different economic circumstances probably limited the full application of this principle, since dividend policy was probably dictated by those in control of the corporation. In many cases no earnings at all were distributed, presumably for reasons of tax avoidance; but these instances do not appear to have been important in the aggregate. In the case of large corporations with wide ownership, the increased distribution of earnings was probably influenced by the desire to reduce corporation taxes *per se*. But this object appeared to be circumscribed by other factors such as the accessibility and cost of securing capital from outside sources, and the desirability of maintaining reserves.

The urgency of conserving corporation assets frequently outweighed the advantages of tax reduction and militated against the distribution of earnings. The working capital of many corporations had been impaired by the ravages of the depression and never fully recovered. In general, those companies with a small distribution of profits had a less favorable liquidity position than those with large distributions. Moreover, the desirability of retaining reserves against the exigencies of business was particularly important to companies subject to serious cyclical fluctuations in profits. Corporations with maturing obligations and fixed interest charges needed to conserve their working capital in order to preserve their solvency; and there is some indication that corporations with a preponderance of debt tended to distribute the least earnings. Growing industries also tended to plow back their profits in order to finance capital requirements. This was also true of companies with heavy investments in inventory, which more or less automatically reinvested profits resulting from the inflationary prices of the period.

On the other hand, the liberality of reserves permitted by the revenue law made it possible for some industries to distribute virtually all their taxable income. Mining and oil companies in particular were favored by the generous allowances made for depletion, which enabled them to reinvest economic income without being subject to the surtax.

LEGAL FACTORS GOVERNING DISTRIBUTION OF EARNINGS

The relief provided corporations with contracts restricting payment of dividends was much criticized for its limited applicability. Nevertheless, the size of credits claimed under the law were rather substantial and amounted to at least 2.0 per cent of the total dividend credits claimed in 1936 and 1937. In relationship to total dividend credits reported, corporations in the middle income classes benefited most from these provisions. Undue hardship may have been experienced by many corporations whose dividends were limited by tacit rather than written agreements with creditors. Because of the chance benefits enjoyed by many corporations with appropriate contracts and the discrimination against those with no less binding but unacceptable agreements, justice would have been better served by a less discriminatory tax rate of, say, one half the full scale, instead of by a complete remission of taxes. This treatment would have been justified by the fact that the stockholders' equity was no less improved in these cases than if earnings were voluntarily retained.

Because of the ease with which an accumulated deficit could be removed in most states, few corporations appeared to be handicapped by various state laws prohibiting payment of dividends when capital was impaired. While the Supreme Court upheld the position taken by the Treasury Department in these cases, the law promoted undesirable corporation practices which tended to impair the position of creditors. Perhaps better policy would have been to allow a carry-forward of losses for a reasonable number of years. The original tax bill provided for full exemption from the undistributed profits tax of corporations with book deficits.

Other discriminations were to be found in the case of insolvent corporations. While those in bankruptcy or receivership were exempted from the surtax, similar consideration was denied corporations operating under extra-legal extension agreements which were often more to be desired than a judicial reorganization. Relief was provided in many of these cases, however, where written agreements expressly limited distribution of earnings.

NON-CASH DIVIDENDS

Avoidance of the undistributed profits tax was accomplished by the use of non-cash taxable dividends, which amounted to over 5 per cent of the total dividend credits claimed. Their importance varied inversely with the size of corporation earnings, and were rather appreciable in the case of corporations with income below $100,000 (about 12 per cent of total dividend credit).

The most important non-cash dividends were in other assets of the corporation, which amounted to over 2½ per cent of the total dividend credits of all corporations. Although the most important form of non-cash distributions by the largest corporations, they were of relatively greater benefit to small companies. Since the assets distributed consisted mostly of investments in other corporations, the corporation suffered little loss of funds essential to the business. Such distributions were also consistent with the objectives of the Administration to eliminate holding companies and to simplify corporate structures. They were largely a temporary relief, however, being limited to the amount of investments possessed.

The second most important form of non-cash dividend was in obligations of the corporation, which amounted to a little over 2 per cent of total dividend credits. Their importance varied inversely with the size of earnings: Giant corporations made virtually no use at all of such obligations. The employment of this type of dividend was dictated largely by the expediency of avoiding taxes without incurring an immediate drain on corporation funds. In postponing the payment of dividends, however, encouragement was given to a financial practice which is rarely sanctioned by sound business principles.

Suprisingly limited use was made of taxable stock dividends, which amounted to less than one per cent of total dividend credits. Their importance varied little with the size of earnings, except that their employment by largest income classes was relatively insignificant. Payment of preferred stock to common stockholders was the most important form of stock dividend used. Considerable use was also made of the optional stock dividend privilege.

Many factors militated against the employment of stock dividends. Perhaps the most important was the uncertainty regarding their eligibility as taxable income: The Supreme Court had previously ruled that common stock dividends paid to common stockholders were not taxable, but had not ruled on the taxability of other types. The great majority of small corporations, for example, appeared to be practically precluded from their use (except in optional form) by the simplicity of their capital structure: Unless preferred stock was already outstanding, the taxation of stock dividends was of doubtful constitutionality. There was also the objection to complicating the capital structure by their use. In the case of non-listed corporations, it was difficult to determine a fair value and no means was provided of paying the income tax on their receipt.

EXTERNAL VERSUS INTERNAL FINANCING OF CAPITAL REQUIREMENTS

The taxation of undistributed profits was urged for the purpose of encouraging the development of a freer capital market. By compelling the distribution of earnings it was believed that the interest of stockholders would be better protected against the arbitrary decision of management to reinvest rather than distribute earnings. In this way, it was claimed, new investment in corporation enterprise would be put to the test of the market and a better allocation of capital would thereby be secured.

A considerable amount of new security offerings was apparently generated by the new tax measure. To the extent that these issues resulted from the disbursement of earnings that otherwise would have been retained, the interests of shareholders were probably better served. But it is impossible to determine whether the direction given to new investment was any better, if, indeed, much different, than it would have been without the distribution of earnings impelled by the surtax. Some salutary influence may have been exercised, however, in deterring expansion plans of questionable merit.

The conventional method of financing the distribution of earnings required for reinvestment was by sale of new stock or bonds to shareholders. This was accomplished by the use of preemptive rights which gave common stockholders the privilege of subscribing to new securities on favorable terms. In the case of new common stock, subscriptions were sold below the market price; in the case of bonds and preferred stock, a favorable conversion privilege was given to make such purchase attractive. An incentive was given to the employment of these techniques during 1936 and 1937 for the purpose of recouping dividends, but the aggregate amount, while substantial, was somewhat less than could be expected.

Many factors limited the practicability of such alternatives to direct reinvestment of earnings. One of the most serious was the cost of flotation of new security issues. Not only was it essential to compensate investment bankers for underwriting their sale (or to pay commission fees to selling agents) but additional costs were incurred in registering new security issues, preparing prospectuses, and paying legal and accounting fees, and taxes. While it was less expensive to sell new securities to stockholders than to the public generally, the cost in many cases discouraged this avenue of avoidance of the undistributed profits tax. This was particularly true of small size issues whose high cost of flotation greatly narrowed the tax differential in favor of distributing earnings.

Other limitations were imposed by market conditions. Successful use of preferential rights is contingent upon the maintenance of an appreciable discount of subscription price below market value. In times of market uncertainty or a declining market, "rights" tended to lose their value, with the result that many issues were unabsorbed or withdrawn. The experience with convertible issues was particularly unfavorable during this period, when many issues were undigested and substantial losses were incurred by underwriters.

EFFECT ON EXPANSION OF SMALL BUSINESS

It is generally recognized that small businesses were handicapped by the undistributed profits tax because of their dependence upon reinvested earnings for growth. The conventional investment banking channels were unavailable for the purpose of raising capital and, when large enough to justify a security issue, the cost was prohibitive. The cost of bank credit was also relatively high.

On the other hand, small corporations enjoyed an advantage over the large corporation in recapturing dividends through the use of quasi-coercive stock rights. Sales of capital stock by very small companies appeared to be rather large. The close community of interest which characterized their ownership and control could facilitate this process with little or no loss of funds. This factor probably largely accounted for the unusually large increase in earnings distributed for purposes of tax avoidance.

The medium size business, however, appeared to be at the most serious disadvantage. Neither large enough to exploit the facilities of the capital market at a reasonable cost, nor small enough to enjoy the advantages of a coordinated dividend-stock subscription plan, the medium size company was probably confronted with the most serious problem of adjustment to the undistributed profits tax.

The specific dividend credit enabled small income companies (with net incomes of $50,000 or less) to retain a substantial portion of their earnings without incurring an undue tax on the amount retained. But, as interpreted by the Treasury Department, the relief proved to be somewhat less than anticipated, and was effectively limited to corporations with an income substantially less than $50,000. Above this income range appreciably less earnings were retained, on the average, but at a substantially higher tax rate than that paid by the smaller income group.

As a result of the superior ability of large companies to finance expansion from external sources, it is believed that the undistributed profits tax tended to promote the growing concentration of industrial control. While it is questionable whether the surtax arrested the development of new monopolies, it tended to strengthen those already in power because of the handicaps imposed on potential competitors dependent upon reinvested earnings for their growth.

3. Technical Criticisms of the Law

Much of the opposition to the undistributed profits tax was directed against particular provisions of the law rather than against its general principles. Even its supporters recognized the need for revision in many respects. Such revision would have made it possible to strengthen the objectives of the Administration without an undue sacrifice of its principles. The major changes that are believed to have been desirable in the interests of equity are summarized below.

LENGTH OF THE ACCOUNTING PERIOD

One of the most serious objections was the arbitrary limitation of taxable income to that realized in the short span of one year. No recognition was given to the net effect of variations in profits and losses over a period of years on the availability of earnings for distribution to shareholders. As a result, not only was capital taxed in many instances but an incentive was given to the distribution of capital rather than real earnings of a corporation. Offset of prior years' losses by a carry-forward provision for a reasonable period of time, say four or five years, would have greatly ameliorated this situation. If this carry-forward were made retroactive, business would have been given an opportunity to restore its working capital depleted by depression losses, cycle-sensitive industries would have been treated more equitably, and many corporations with an accumulated deficit enabled to repair their legal capital. While subject to some administrative difficulties, there was ample precedent in the carry-forward provisions of the previous tax laws, which had been repealed in 1933. The Revenue Act of 1938 permitted a dividend credit for the loss of the previous year, but the carry-forward provision was not restored for corporation normal taxes until 1939.

THE DIVIDEND PERIOD

Similarly, extension of the dividend period beyond the fiscal year would have eliminated much of the guess work from dividend payments necessary to avoid the surtax. As it was, earnings for the year had to be estimated in advance of the close of the fiscal period, and any underestimates were subject to a penalty tax, starting at 7 per cent. The original bill allowed credit for dividends paid two and one-half months after the close of the period.

CONCEPT OF TAXABLE INCOME

More realistic treatment of inventory profits and losses would have removed serious objections by many companies to the pressure on distribution of taxable income required to carry larger investment in inventories due to rising prices. Distribution of such fictitious profits made many corporations vulnerable to loss through subsequent price decline. Recognition was given to this problem in 1938 by the liberalization of inventory valuation methods.

On the other hand, liberal depletion allowances based on percentage of gross receipts or discovery value gave an undue advantage to oil, gas, and mining companies generally. The allowance of depletion in excess of cost for purposes of the undistributed profits tax greatly improved the advantage already given these companies under the normal tax. The surtax privilege could have reasonably been avoided without impairing incentives to new discovery and exploration.

Full allowance of capital losses for purposes of the undistributed profits tax would have better recognized the availability of earnings for distribution.

THE RATE STRUCTURE

Complete elimination of the corporation normal tax would have resulted in windfall profits to many corporations which distributed their earnings in full. However, consideration probably should have been given to reduction of the normal tax over a period of time so that only undistributed profits would have been taxed and more complete integration of the corporation income tax with the individual income tax achieved.

More important, perhaps, was the size of the graduation in the surtax rate itself. While only a corporation surtax rate equal to the highest individual surtax rate would have achieved full equality of individual and corporation taxes, such a high rate was recognized as being prohibitive. Reduction of the initial rate of 7 per cent to a more nominal rate of 2 or 3 per cent, or even zero, for the first 20 or 30 per cent of corporation earnings, would have permitted reasonable retention of profits without undue sacrifice of the principles of the tax; beyond this point, however, more effective compulsion would have been given to distribution of earnings by a sharply increased graduated rate schedule up to a maximum of, say, 50 per cent, instead of 27 per cent.

TREATMENT OF INTEREST ON FUNDED DEBT

Net income available for distribution was determined after deduction of bond interest and other fixed charges in conformity with the traditional concept of normal tax net income. Determination of net income *before* bond interest charges, and allowances of a credit for their payment, would have been not only justified in principle but would have served a practical purpose in alleviating the burden of the surtax on many debt-ridden corporations in reducing the surtax rates applicable to undistributed earnings. Such policy would not have exercized much, if any, compulsion on the distribution of corporation earnings since interest payments are rarely discretionary with management. However, bonds are employed as an alternative method of financing capital requirements where it is desirable to "trade on the equity," enlarge the source of funds, and for other reasons. Since the fixed interest charges represent in reality a prior contractual claim to earnings, credit for bond interest payments would have realized more uniformity in treatment of corporations following different financial plans.

DOUBLE TAXATION OF EARNINGS

In one other respect the undistributed profits tax held a possibility of inequitable treatment of shareholders through the double taxation of corporation profits. Although failure to pay dividends in one year would subject the corporation to a compensatory tax, subsequent distribution of these earnings would expose the stockholders to their taxation under the personal income tax. This would be particularly true of the taxation of accumulated arrears paid on preferred stock which for various reasons the directors may have not seen fit to distribute in the year earned.

OTHER PROVISIONS

Many other recommendations made at the time would have emasculated the tax measure. Credit allowed for repayment of debt, for example, would have permitted corporations to escape taxes simply by the liquidation of short term loans undertaken in the normal course of business to finance seasonal and cyclical peaks of production and marketing. Proposals to allow credit for profits reinvested in capital goods were not only inconsistent with the rationale of the tax, and would have utterly destroyed its effectiveness, but were also impracticable in application.

4. General Economic Effects

EFFECT ON SAVINGS AND CONSUMPTION

The taxation of undistributed profits contributed to a substantial change in the flow of income saved and spent on consumption goods. As a result of the initial impact of the tax, corporation savings were reduced by an estimated $1.4 billion a year. Approximately $0.4 billion of this was diverted to the Federal government through taxes paid both by the corporation (on retained income) and by individuals on their increased income. It is estimated that about one-half the remaining $1.0 billion was saved and one-half spent on consumption goods and services. Total savings of the economy were accordingly reduced by approximately $0.9 billion. However, only part of this reduction in savings can be attributed to the particular form of the tax: Had an equivalent amount of revenue been derived from a direct tax on corporation incomes, total savings would have been reduced by approximately the amount of the tax—$0.4 billion. The taxation of undistributed profits, therefore, enhanced consumer expenditures by an estimated half billion dollars more than would probably have been realized from the most logical alternative form of tax.

LONG-RUN EFFECT ON NATIONAL INCOME

In the long run, a reduction in proportion of the national income saved was probably conducive to a higher level of national income. Failure of new investment to keep pace with the high propensity to save appeared to be one of the fundamental factors accounting for the under-employment of resources during the 1930's. By reducing the proportion of the national income saved, the new tax policy tended to raise the general level of purchasing power and thereby to bring about a better equilibrium of savings with new investment. The taxation of savings, therefore, appears to have been compatible with the secular decline in new investment experienced during this period. In this respect the undistributed profits tax contributed to a higher potential level of employment and national income. On the other hand, new investment may have actually been discouraged by the tax on retained income. While a substantial part of new capital requirements was supplied by the capital market, it is very questionable if the external sources of capital entirely replaced the earnings distributed by business as a result of the surtax. Large corporations evidenced little general curtailment in new investment but small and medium size businesses were at a disadvantage in securing funds for growth.

CYCLICAL EFFECTS

The taxation of undistributed profits probably intensifies the short cyclical swings of business. By enhancing consumer purchasing power during the upswing of a cycle, additional stimulus is given to increased investment in plant capacity and in inventories. The reduction in savings tends to impair the resistance of the economy to cyclical change and to increase the amplitude of fluctuations in prices and wages. This situation is facilitated by the expansion of bank credit which supplies the gap between the planned investment and real savings of the economy. To the extent that the undistributed profits tax diverts retained earnings to the purchase of consumer goods, new investment tends to be financed by inflationary means. While it may be argued that expansion is deterred by the taxation of corporation savings, it seems likely that such reduction is more than offset by the general stimulus given by the enlarged purchasing power.

Subsequent reaction on the down-swing might, therefore, be correspondingly greater. Because of the reduction in corporation reserves, business expenditures would be curtailed to a greater extent by the necessity of liquidating bank loans and other debts incurred to finance the increased volume of business during the up-swing. The increased distribution of earnings would tend to impair the "cushion" of corporations against losses and to introduce a greater risk of failure. Finally, the compulsion to distribute earnings in good years would make less available for distribution in a business recession. While the maintenance of dividends and wages has been greatly exaggerated as a factor in business stability, the undistributed profits tax would, nevertheless, tend to have a perverse effect in this respect.

It is impossible to isolate the effect of the undistributed profits tax on the business recession of 1937-1938. Its effects on savings and investment were largely cancelled out by increased taxes on payrolls which impinged on consumption. While this decline in business activity was one of the most precipitous on record, it was of short duration. Moreover, dividend payments in 1938 were not less than expected despite the claim that corporation funds were drained by unusually large dividend payments in the preceding two years. It is possible, however, that retention of the surtax on undistributed profits might have delayed business recovery and it was largely on account of this fear that the tax was repealed in 1938.

5. Alternative Approaches to the Taxation of Undistributed Profits

There are many alternative methods of achieving a better coordination of income taxes on corporations and their shareholders. One general category would assess the tax on the shareholders, the other would impose the levy at the corporate level. All of them are subject in varying degrees to limitations on economic, equitable or administrative grounds.[1] One method, called the " capital-gains " approach, would eliminate the corporation tax and retain only a tax on capital gains realized from the sale, gift or devolution at death of capital stock.[2] This plan would permit too generous postponement of taxes into the indefinite future, and would allow too much latitude for tax avoidance by selection of the most appropriate time for transfer. Another method, called the " partnership " approach would tax, so far as practicable, the pro rata share of corporation profits distributable to the shareholders whether paid out or not.[3] While employed in Great Britain and Australia for " private " corporations, this method would present almost insuperable administrative difficulties in the case of large widely owned corporations. Moreover, the individual taxpayer would be confronted with the problem of paying taxes on income that was not actually received. A combination of these

1 For an excellent analysis of the rationale and administrative problems of these various proposals see Richard B. Goode, *The Postwar Corporation Tax Structure*, Division of Tax Research, U. S. Treasury Department, Washington, D. C., December, 1946.

2 See Henry C. Simons, *Personal Income Taxation* (Chicago: University of Chicago Press, 1938), Chapters VII and IX; William Vickrey, "A Reasonable Undistributed Profits Tax," *Taxes*, Vol. 23 (Feb., 1945), pp. 123-127. In order to offset the tax savings from reinvestment of earnings, the latter proposal would supplement the capital gains tax with a recurrent low rate of tax on accumulated undistributed earnings for every year retained.

3 *Final Report of the Committee of the National Tax Association on Federal Taxation of Corporations*, Robert Murray Haig, Chairman, *Proceedings* of the National Tax Association, 1939, p. 555.

two approaches is the so-called "inventory" method which would tax the distributable share of earnings of non-listed corporations as well as *unrealized* gains in market value of listed stocks owned by the taxpayer (in addition to realized capital gains).[4] This plan is subject to the same limitations as the partnership plan.

Three other methods have been more or less successfully attempted in the United States. One of these is the penalty tax imposed on undue accumulation of profits, still in effect through Section 102 of the Internal Revenue Code. It has limited applicability, however, and derives its force from administrative review of each situation with respect to the intent to avoid personal income taxes. The "dividend-received" credit technique was employed in the United States prior to 1936. This provided for exemption from the individual normal tax of dividends received. Reinstitution of this tax credit device with extension of the credit to the first bracket income tax rate, has been recommended as a solution to the problem of so-called double taxation of corporation income.[5] The other method of a "compensatory" tax on undistributed profits is the subject of the present study. A slight variation of this method which would allow a tax credit to the corporation for dividends paid, similar to the device employed in 1938 and 1939, has also been suggested.[6]

4 *Facing the Tax Problem*, Carl Shoup, Roy Blough, Mabel Newcomer, Research Directors (New York: The Twentieth Century Fund), 1937, pp. 477-478.

5 *A Tax Program for a Solvent America*, Committee on Postwar Tax Policy, Roswell Magill, Chairman (New York, 1945), pp. 98-103.

6 Richard B. Goode, *op. cit.*, pp. 37-46. Revival of the undistributed profits tax at a rate of about 16 per cent has been proposed by Beardsley Ruml and H. Christian Sonne, *Fiscal and Monetary Policy*, National Planning Association, Pamphlet No. 35, July, 1944. Mr. Sonne has more recently advocated an additional high surtax of 60 per cent on any earnings retained in excess of 25 per cent or $50,000 whichever is higher. *How Should Corporations be Taxed?* Symposium conducted by the Tax Institute, Inc. (New York, 1947), pp. 19-30.

The plan which appears to hold the most promise, however, is the British withholding method.[7] While full equality would not be achieved between corporation tax rates and taxes on individual incomes at all levels of income, the withholding method appears to offer the best prospects of achieving a substantial improvement in equity without imposing undue hardships on corporations and without immoderate administrative difficulties.

The British system withholds from the corporation a standard rate of tax on net income (50 per cent during the war years). The shareholder is required to add the tax applicable to dividends received in computing his personal income tax liability and is entitled to a credit for such taxes paid at the source in settling his account with the government. Thus, he may recoup any taxes withheld from the corporation in excess of his personal income tax liability on dividend income, by a refund from the government. Additional surtaxes, if any, are payable on any increased assessment.

The particular superiority of the British system over a dividend paid credit plan with a comparable rate of tax lies in the absence of compulsion to distribute earnings within the year earned. While undistributed profits are subject to the standard rate of tax withheld from the corporation, and the incentive to distribute earnings would be little affected, the opportunity of securing the tax credit would extend indefinitely into the future (unless a limit were imposed). The corporation would thereby have a better opportunity to correlate its dividend policy with the changing conditions of the capital market, and generally would be better able to follow a flexible financial plan. It is true

7 This plan has been recommended for adoption in the United States by the Committee for Economic Development, *A Postwar Federal Tax Plan for High Employment*, 1944. See also Harold M. Groves, *Postwar Taxation and Economic Progress* (New York: McGraw-Hill Book Co., 1946), pp. 40-73 for a defense of this system. George E. Barnes, "A Plan to Simplify Corporation Taxes," *Exchange*, Vol. V, Sept., 1944, proposes the adoption of a withholding plan to be superimposed on a normal corporation "franchise" tax.

that better opportunity would also be given to minimization of taxes over a period of time, but the tax loss would probably not be too great a price to pay for the improvement in business stability.

Additional administrative problems would be introduced if it were not believed desirable to follow the British policy of ignoring changes in the withholding rate between two different periods. Since tax credit is allowed at the current standard withholding rate, benefit would be given to the shareholder if the tax was actually withheld at a lower rate. Some problems would arise in the treatment of tax exempt income (with which Great Britain is not concerned) as well as in the treatment of preferred dividends, intercorporate dividends, and other minor matters. An intensive study of the problems has convinced the author that a flat rate of tax can be easily administered through the present withholding machinery without the necessity of corporations' filing individual reports on dividend recipients. [8]

8 See paper presented by the author at the meeting of the National Tax Association, November, 1947, "Alternative Methods of Taxing Corporate Earnings at the Personal Level: The Withholding Approach," *Proceedings of the Annual Tax Conference, 1947.*

SELECTED BIBLIOGRAPHY

Books and Monographs

Altman, Oscar. *Savings, Investment and National Income.* Temporary National Economic Committee. Monograph No. 37, Washington, 1941.

Angell, James W. *Investment and Business Cycles.* New York: McGraw-Hill Book Co., 1941.

Blakey, Roy G. and Gladys C. *The Federal Income Tax.* New York: Longmans, Green & Co., 1940.

Bonbright, James C. *The Valuation of Property.* New York: McGraw-Hill Book Co., 1937.

Buehler, Alfred G. *The Undistributed Profits Tax.* New York: McGraw-Hill Book Co., 1937.

Buchanan, Norman S. *The Economics of Corporate Enterprise.* New York: Henry Holt and Co., 1940.

Clark, John M. *Strategic Factors in Business Cycles.* New York: National Bureau of Economic Research, 1934.

Colm, Gerhard and Lehman, Fritz. *Economic Consequences of Recent American Tax Policy.* Social Research, Supplement, 1938.

Committee on Postwar Tax Policy, Roswell Magill, Chairman. *A Tax Program for a Solvent America.* New York, 1945.

Curry, O. J. *Utilization of Corporate Profits in Prosperity and Depression.* Michigan Business Studies, IX, No. 4. Ann Arbor, Michigan, 1941.

Dennison, H. S.; Filene, Lincoln; Flanders, Ralph E.; Leeds, Morris E. *Toward Full Employment.* New York: McGraw-Hill Book Co., 1938.

Goode, Richard B. *The Postwar Corporation Tax Structure.* U. S. Treasury Department, Washington, 1946.

Graham, Benjamin and Dodd, David L. *Security Analysis.* New York: McGraw-Book Co., 1940.

Groves, Harold M. *Postwar Taxation and Economic Progress.* New York: McGraw-Hill Book Co., 1946.

Guthmann, Harry G. and Dougall, Herbert E. *Corporate Financial Policy.* New York: Prentice-Hall, Inc., 1940.

Haven, T. Kenneth. *Investment Banking Under the Securities and Exchange Commission.* Michigan Business Studies, IX, No. 3, 1940. University of Michigan, Ann Arbor.

Hansen, Alvin H. *Fiscal Policy and Business Cycles.* New York: W. W.. Norton & Co., Inc., 1941.

Hynning, Clifford J. *Taxation of Corporate Enterprise.* Monograph No. 9. Temporary National Economic Committee. Washington, 1941.

Kendrick, M. Slade. *The Undistributed Profits Tax.* Washington: The Brookings Institution, 1937.

Keynes, John M. *The General Theory of Employment, Interest and Money.* New York: Harcourt, Brace & Co., 1936.

Lutz, Friedrich A. *Corporate Cash Balances*. New York: National Bureau of Economic Research, 1945.

Magill, Roswell F. *Taxable Income*. New York: The Ronald Press Co., 1936.

Magill, R., Parker, L. H., and King, E. P. *A Summary of the British Tax System*, printed for the use of the Joint Committee on Internal Revenue Taxation. Washington, 1935.

Marple, Raymond P. *Capital Surplus and Corporate Net Worth*. New York: The Ronald Press, 1936.

Merwin, Charles L. *Financial Characteristics of American Manufacturing Corporations*. Monograph No. 15. Temporary National Economic Committee. Washington, 1941.

—— *Financing Small Corporations*. New York: National Bureau of Economic Research, 1942.

National Tax Association. *Preliminary Report of Committee on Federal Taxation of Corporations*, Robert M. Haig, Chairman, 1938.

—— *Final Report of Committee on Federal Taxation of Corporations*, Robert M. Haig, Chairman, 1939.

Paul, Randolph E. *Taxation for Prosperity*. Indianapolis: Bobbs-Merrill, 1947.

Seligman, E. R. A. *Essays in Taxation*, 10th Ed. New York: The Macmillan Co., 1925.

—— *The Income Tax*. New York: The Macmillan Co., 1921.

Simons, Henry C. *Personal Income Taxation*. Chicago: University of Chicago Press, 1938.

Taitel, Martin. *Profits, Productive Activities and New Investment*. Monograph No. 12. Temporary National Economic Committee, Washington. 1941.

Tax Policy League, Symposium. *How Shall Business Be Taxed?* New York: Tax Policy League, 1937.

Tax Institute Symposium. *How Should Corporations Be Taxed?* New York: Tax Institute, Inc., 1947.

Twentieth Century Fund, Inc. *Facing the Tax Problem*. New York, 1937.

—— *How Profitable is Big Business?* New York, 1937.

Tugwell, Rexford G. *The Industrial Discipline and the Government Arts*. New York: Columbia University Press, 1933.

ARTICLES

Abramovitz, Moses. "Savings and Investments: Profits vs. Prosperity?" *American Economic Review, Supplement*, XXXII, No. 2, Part 2 (June, 1942), 53-88.

Adams, T. S. "Federal Taxes Upon Income and Excess Profits," *American Economic Review*, Supplement, VIII (1920), 15-18.

——. "Fundamental Problems of Federal Income Taxation," *Quarterly Journal of Economics*, XXXV (1921), 527-56.

Alvord, Ellsworth C. "Current Trends in Federal Finances and Taxation," *The Tax Magazine*, XV (June, 1937), 315-323.

Anderson, Harold C. "The Taxability of Dividends," *The Tax Magazine*, XV (February, 1937), 74-78.

Colm, Gerhard. "Conflicting Theories of Corporate Income Taxation," *Law and Contemporary Problems*, VII, No. 2. Duke University, N. C. (1940), 281-290.

Columbia Law Review. "The Corporate Undistributed Profits Tax," XXXVI (1936), 1321-1354.

Derrickson, Gardner F. "The Trend of Corporate Profits," *Survey of Current Business* (April, 1946), 9-20.

Edwards, R. S., and Black, D. "Notes on the British Income Tax and Company Reserves," *Review of Economic Studies* (Feb., 1938).

Humphrey, Don D. "The Relation of Surpluses to Income and Employment during Depression," *American Economic Review*, XXVIII (June, 1936), 223-234.

Fortune, Round Table. "Taxation and Recovery," XIX (May, 1938), 67-68; 110-129.

Gilbert, D. W. "Should the Undistributed Profits Tax be Repealed?" *The Tax Magazine* (Dec., 1936), 710-711; 755-756.

——. "Undistributed Profits and Business Fluctuations," *Taxes* (Feb., 1938), 72-74.

Graham, Benjamin. "The Undistributed Profits Tax and the Investor," *Yale Law Journal*, XLVI (1936), 1-18.

Harvard Law Journal. "The Surtax on Undistributed Profits," L (1936), 332-344.

Hendricks, H. "The Surtax on Undistributed Profits of Corporations," *Yale Law Journal*, XLVI (1936), 19-51.

Kent, Arthur H. "The Federal Revenue Act of 1936—Some Current Problems," *The Tax Magazine*, XV (April, 1937), 204-208.

McIntyre, Francis. "The Effect of the Undistributed Profits Tax upon the Distribution of Corporate Earnings—A Statistical Appraisal," *Econometrica*, Vol. VII, No. 3 (July, 1939).

McLaren, Norman L. "Management of Capital Distribution Under the Revenue Act of 1936," *Journal of Accountancy*, LXII (1936), 334-357.

Montgomery, R. H. "The Tax on Undistributed Income," *Harvard Business Review*, XV (1936), 19-28.

Nelson, Godfrey, N. "The Taxation of Corporate Surplus," *The Tax Magazine*, XV (January, 1937), 15-19.

Rolbein, David L. "Non-Cash Dividends and Stock Rights as Methods for Avoidance of the Undistributed Profits Tax," *The Journal of Business of the University of Chicago*, XII, No. 3 (July, 1939), 221-264.

Schulman, Walter H. "Undistributed Profits Tax Avoidance after the Koshland Case," *The Tax Magazine*, XIV (December, 1936), 703-705.

Seidman, F. E. "Dividend Policy under the Undistributed Profits Tax." *Commercial and Financial Chronicle*, Vol. 143. p. 3213.

Seidman, Frank P. "The Undistributed Profits Tax—Suggested Changes in the Law," *The Tax Magazine*, XV (Feb., 1937), 79-82.

Seidman, J. S. "Undistributed Profits Tax Problems," *The Tax Magazine*, XIV (August, 1936), 453-55.

Seltzer, Lawrence H. "The Undistributed Profits Tax," Address before School of Business Administration, University of Michigan (May 8, 1937).

Smith, James G. "Economic Significance of the Undistributed Profits Tax," *American Economic Review*, XXVIII (June, 1938), 303-310.

Straub, Walter A. "Corporate Policy Trends Resulting from the Undistributed Earnings Tax," *Financial Management Series*, No. 51. New York: American Management Association, 1937.

Tebeau, R. L. "Cost of Surplus Profits Tax to Large and Small Corporations," *Dun's Review*, Vol. 46 (Jan. 1938), 21-23.

Thorp, Willard L. and George, Edwin B. "An Appraisal of the Undistributed Profits Tax," *Dun's Review*, Vol. 45 (Sept., 1937), 5-36.

Vickrey, William. "A Reasonable Undistributed Profits Tax," *Taxes*, XXIII (Feb., 1945), 123-27.

Weidenhammer, R. "Faulty Investment of Corporate Savings," *American Economic Review*, XXIII (1933), 35-41.

Official Documents

Great Britain. *Report of the Committee on National Debt and Taxation*. Cmd. 2800, London: H. M. Stationery Office, 1927.

Revenue Act of 1936. Public No. 740, 74th Cong., 2d Sess., 1936.

Securities and Exchange Commission. *Data on Certain Common Stock Issues Registered Under the Securities Act of 1933 and Offered to Stockholders by Means of Rights*, Statistical Series Release No. 41, Item I, November, 1937.

——. *Cost of Flotation for Registered Securities, 1938-1939*. Washington, D. C., March, 1941.

——. *Sales Record of Unseasoned Registered Securities, 1933-1938*. Washington, D. C., June, 1941.

Temporary National Economic Committee on the Concentration of Economic Power in the United States. *Savings and Investment, Hearings*, Part 9, May 16-26, 1939. Washington, D. C., 1940.

——. *Final Report of the Executive Secretary*. Washington, D. C., 1941.

U. S. House of Representatives, Committee on Ways and Means. *Hearings on Revenue Act, 1936*, 74th Cong., 2d Sess., March 30–April 7, 1936.

——. *Hearings on Revenue Revision, 1938*, 75th Cong., 3d Sess., January 14-25, 1938.

U. S. Senate, Committee on Finance. *Hearings on HR 12395, Revenue Act, 1936*, 74th Cong., 2d Sess., April 30–May 12, 1936.

——. *Hearings on HR 9682, Revenue Act, 1938*, 75th Cong., 3d Sess., March 17-22, 1938.

U. S. Treasury Department. *Bulletin of the Treasury Department*, February, 1940; January, 1943.

——. Bureau of Internal Revenue. *Statistics of Income; Statistics of Income Source Book.*

——. *Regulations 94. Income Tax, Revenue Act*, 1936.

Works Progress Administration. *Statistics of American Listed Corporations*, 2 Parts. Sponsored by the Securities and Exchange Commission, December, 1940.

INDEX

Bei Fragen zur Produktsicherheit wenden Sie sich bitte an:
If you have any questions regarding product safety,
please contact:

Walter de Gruyter GmbH
Genthiner Straße 13
10785 Berlin
productsafety@degruyterbrill.com